ALL
RIGHT
NOW

ALL
RIGHT
NOW

FINDING CONSENSUS
on ETHICAL QUESTIONS

TIMOTHY J. GEDDERT

Herald Press
Scottdale, Pennsylvania
Waterloo, Ontario

Library of Congress Cataloging-in-Publication Data
Geddert, Timothy J.
  [Verantwortlich Leben. English]
  All right now : finding consensus on ethical questions / by Timothy J.
Geddert.
      p. cm.
  Includes bibliographical references.
  ISBN 978-0-8361-9418-0 (pbk. : alk. paper)
  1. Ethics in the Bible. I. Title.
  BS2417.E8G4313 2008
  241–dc22
                                                    2008013746

ALL RIGHT NOW
Library of Congress Catalog Card Number: 2008013746
International Standard Book Number: 978-0-8361-9418-0
Printed in the United States of America
Book design by Joshua Byler
Cover by Greg Yoder
Photo from iStockphoto

Originally published as *Verantwortlich Leben: Wenn Christen sich entscheiden müssen* by Neufeld Verlag (Schwarzenfeld, Germany), 2004, second edition 2007.

13 12 11 10 09 08   10 9 8 7 6 5 4 3 2 1

To order or request information please call 1-800-759-4447
or visit www.heraldpress.com.

*Dedicated to all those people
with whom I have been able to experience
"Where two or three are gathered together
in Jesus' name,
there he is in the midst of them."*

Contents

Foreword by Peter Strauch 9
Preface 13

Part 1: Basics
1. God Speaks Through the Bible: 19
   Why Do We Hear God Differently?
2. Matthew 18: 45
   Reconciliation and Mutual Accountability
3. What Constitutes a Biblical Ethic? 63

Part 2: Examples
4. Love Your Enemies 79
5. Sexuality 95
6. Divorce and Remarriage .125
7. Homosexuality 143
8. Money and Possessions 169

Part 3: Attitudes
9. 'It Has Seemed Good to the Holy Spirit' 187
10. Two Sons and a Running Father 201
11. A Pile of Stones or a Word of Grace 213

Bottom Lines 223

Notes 227
The Author 229

Foreword

The book you have just opened is a surprising book—perhaps an unusual book. You might even be irritated by it. On the following pages you will encounter many different themes, and not only that: the way in which Tim Geddert comes alongside the reader is also unusual. At times he shares principles, then he interprets Bible texts, and then again he shows how he works with and answers very difficult questions.

But in spite of everything, you will no doubt experience this book as I did. You will learn to know an author who begins to dialogue with you and then to think step by step with you through topics that responsible Christians cannot dodge: love of enemies, sexuality, marriage and divorce, homosexuality, and money and possessions. These are all areas that challenge us and for which we need to find answers. I don't mean we need to memorize someone else's list of answers; I mean we need personal answers, carefully thought through and grounded in Scripture. And that is what happens here.

I consider this an important book, and I will gladly tell you why.

I have worked primarily with youth and young adults for many years. Many of them come from Christian homes; they've known the Bible since childhood but have never learned how to live with the Bible. Above all they have never experienced God's good news about life as something that brings freedom. Their pious Christian background consisted of numerous rules, often formulated negatively: You shall not! You are not allowed to . . .

That has deeply influenced them, and because of this many have never learned how to be truly glad about their faith in Jesus Christ. Even when they experience beautiful and pleasant things, they can't get rid of the feeling that somewhere there must be a catch, that somehow things are going too well, and they are at least in danger of losing the seriousness of their life with God. For them, being a Christian is mostly about foregoing things. Whenever they stand at a fork in the road, they assume from the start that the harder road is the one God wants them to take. Not everyone I have come to know has been able to hang on to this brand of religion for the long haul. Some slipped away inwardly. They were still formally present, but in reality they were not there anymore. They simply lived their own lives. Others publicly announced they were calling it quits with their faith. Some rather demonstratively, others less so, broke free of their religious background and tried to catch up on all the things they had missed out on.

I have also learned to know another kind of Christian. They live a "liberal piety" in which God's grace becomes a cheap thing: whatever we do, grace will take care of it. For these people, God becomes a loveable Lord who closes both eyes when we do wrong and couldn't possibly be upset with anyone. For such people the biblical commands belong to a time-bound system of morals with virtually no meaning for us today. Only love still counts, and nothing that happens in love can really be wrong. In this way there is justification for every divorce and understanding for moral lapses of every kind.

I have been involved with both types of young people, and I've experienced both kinds among older people as well. In terms of their thinking, the older ones were little different from the younger ones. They didn't show it quite as openly, perhaps. Maybe they were more sensitive to their context, less daring in openly breaking with the system in which they had grown up and still felt at home.

What I have come to realize is that both the legalistic and the liberal approaches grow from the same root: an inherited system of rules that is miles away from being freely bound to Jesus in trusting commitment. It is not as though people avoid biblical terms like *freedom* and *joy*. Rather, it is similar to what happened in the former East Germany. There was a great deal of talk about freedom there too, even though it was not really known. It's true that we talk about something most when we have it least.

Empty slogans and pat answers will never break people free from a fossilized Christianity. If someone wants to combat liberal piety by imposing strong rules, the harvest will be just the opposite. It will do no good for parents, church elders, and pastors to keep telling people, "That's not right!" What we need is a faith with foundations, one that does not push aside contemporary questions and controversies, one that in fact draws us in and can show, precisely in the light of such challenges, what the Reformation principle *sola Scriptura* (the Scriptures alone) means.

That is exactly what happens in this book. Tim Geddert doesn't hide the fact that even "the Scriptures alone" needs interpreting and is perhaps more ambiguous than we might have imagined. Isn't it true that the Bible contains time-conditioned teachings? Can we really take over and apply one-to-one everything we find in Scripture? What can help us avoid randomness and inconsistency when we make decisions about the application of Scripture? The author carefully works with these questions. He takes us with him into an analysis of the problems and leads us to well-considered answers.

What especially fascinates me about this book is the path along which Geddert leads the reader. He is teaching us to do our own work. His approach is a model. We all need to learn to travel the necessary paths and to find well-founded answers.

I've noticed something else in this book: we live in an individualistic age. This societal trend does not stop at the door of the church: "My God and I, . . . others have nothing to say to us." Geddert sees that differently because the Bible does. According to his understanding, "fellowship" with brothers and sisters belongs in the life of a Christian. What does that mean? How does that work itself out when we ask about God's will? And what does fellowship really mean when someone falls into sin? How will we as a community deal with it? These are all important and unavoidable questions for those seeking a genuine faith. That is what this book is all about.

This book is not a simple book to digest. It challenges us to work with the author. Sometimes readers have the feeling they are sitting beside the author and together with him probing the questions and looking for the contours of a genuine and fulfilling faith. The suggestions for further thought and discussion help us along the way—personally and with others. I am convinced that those who are willing to be led into the process will make progress in their life with Jesus. Will you let yourself in on it?

Many years ago I was conversing with a young man at the door of a church just before the service began. He told me with disappointment that in his church there was no one that awoke within him the wish "to be like that person." It turned out he was being too negative, that I will admit. Still I am convinced that we need such people—genuine Christians who orient their lives, not merely around following or ignoring traditional rules, but rather by living with Jesus from the foundation up, hearing his word and doing his will. This book will help you to be that kind of person.

Peter Strauch
German Evangelical Alliance
Witten
Easter 2004

Preface

This book aims to offer concrete help to Christian communities as they struggle with ethical questions and try to determine appropriate ethical guidelines. It seeks to find a middle way between a rule-oriented approach, in which everything is viewed legalistically and objectively, and an irresponsible freedom, in which everything is permissible and Christians are responsible to no one for their choices. How exactly can the Bible help us with these matters? This is a major consideration in each chapter of this book. I will not use these questions as an opportunity to push my own ethical views or defend my convictions against the alternatives; my goal is to help readers reach their own conclusions and find common convictions and guidelines in the context of their own Christian community.

So, what is this book about? It is divided into three parts.

Part 1: Basics

- In chapter 1, I aim to reveal how I personally approach the Scriptures. Not every pious-sounding opinion about the Bible helps us to find guidance from the Scriptures. So, what convictions about the nature of Scripture help us? I also address even more basic questions: What kind of book is the Bible? Which goals, which approaches, and which interpretive steps help us make progress in our attempts to understand it?
- Chapter 2 examines Matthew 18, a chapter presenting Jesus' portrayal of the discipleship community. This chapter shows what it means for Jesus to be in our midst and for rec-

onciliation and mutual accountability to characterize our common life.

- In chapter 3, I present twelve points designed to characterize a biblical ethic.

Part 2: Examples

- Each of the next five chapters studies a significant ethical issue and attempts to deal faithfully with biblical texts by reflecting on how the believing community can respond appropriately to them. Chapter 4 examines a text within Jesus' Sermon on the Mount and addresses topics like nonviolence, love of enemies, and the ever-controversial issue of military participation.

- Sexuality is one of God's gifts to humanity. God's instructions on the use of this gift occupy chapter 5. In contemporary society, more and more people assume that an active sexual life is a normal and acceptable component of a love relationship between unmarried people. But what does the Bible say about that? And how should the church respond to the diversity of views that people hold?

- Divorce and remarriage, studied in chapter 6, are not merely abstract topics. They are real life issues for many people, including Christians. How does the Bible help us find answers for some of the difficult questions that surround these issues? How does Scripture provide help for people in difficult marriage relationships or for those whose marriages have failed?

- Chapter 7 deals with homosexuality—a topic about which many people have become insecure. It aims to provide a fair and honest assessment of what the Bible does and does not say about homosexuality, so that we can avoid simplistic, unpersuasive, and one-sided arguments. The goal is to help churches reach a healthy biblical assessment of current societal changes and develop appropriate Christian responses.

- As Christians we confess that all we are and all we have belong to God. But what are the implications of saying that our money, our resources, and our influence are truly God's? How can we learn to serve God and not Mammon? Chapter 8 provides tools to help churches discuss creatively and openly appropriate applications of biblical teaching on this important topic.

Part 3: Attitudes

- Chapter 9 examines Acts 15 and looks to the early church for insight regarding community decision making. The early church was also confronted with difficult questions. How were they able to preserve unity and in the end say, "It has seemed good to the Holy Spirit and to us" (v. 28)? A set of guidelines drawn from Acts 15 can guide us when we are confronted with difficult questions today.
- In the well-known story of the prodigal son (Luke 15:11-32), Jesus reveals God's highest priority: relationships. He shows us how far God is willing to go to rebuild relationships that have broken down. This impressive parable will occupy us in chapter 10.
- Finally, in chapter 11, we examine the episode in which Jesus stands alongside an adulteress woman condemned by legalistic judges (John 8:2-11). Can churches learn from this story how to choose the risk of grace over the security of legalism?

The goal of all this is to encourage churches to think biblically when confronted with difficult ethical questions. What would Jesus have done? What does the Bible teach? How can we find biblical guidance? How can we grow as a responsible "binding and loosing" fellowship of disciples? How does a life that pleases God look? How can we find the best way to live responsibly, in a way that preserves both norms and freedom?

I wish all readers joy in reading and working through this book, and I wish all churches successful experiences as they consider the proposals in this book and then either adopt them or improve on them.

Timothy J. Geddert
Fresno, California
Summer 2008

Part 1
Basics

How often have you stared in disbelief as someone defended an opinion on an ethical matter that seemed obviously wrong to you. Then, to top it off, the person claimed to be basing his or her view on Scripture? How often have you responded in astonishment as you heard that there are churches openly affirming practices that to you are obviously sinful, or perhaps denouncing as sinful other practices that to you seem obviously appropriate and good? And what do you make of issues that so divide churches that each side is convinced that the other is being unfaithful?

My personal conviction is that these situations will continue to baffle and frustrate us as long as we launch directly into discussions of specific ethical questions while remaining unaware that our most significant disagreements are much more basic. Sometimes we do simply disagree about what the Bible says, but more often our real disagreement is about how the Scriptures should guide our ethical thinking. Sometimes we disagree in our personal convictions, but more often our real disagreement is about what role, if any, the church community should play in shaping our convictions and in holding us accountable.

The first section of this book aims to address basic issues like biblical hermeneutics, community discernment, and ethical principles. It is designed to prepare us to deal helpfully with the concrete examples discussed in part 2.

1

God Speaks Through the Bible:

Why Do We Hear God Differently?

In the first chapter I describe how I personally approach the Scriptures. Not every pious-sounding opinion about the Bible will necessarily help us to find guidance from the Scriptures. So, what convictions about the nature of Scripture will help us? I also address even more basic questions: What kind of book is the Bible? Which goals, approaches, and interpretive steps can help us make progress in our attempts to understand the Bible?

The Middle Way

There are many Christians and many churches that would like to throw away all faith traditions of the past, recklessly and uncritically. "Out with the old, in with the new," they declare, and they are quick to adopt almost any cultural fad. The Bible is quoted when it serves to support current trends, and it is shoved aside or seriously misinterpreted when it challenges what we want to do and think. When this happens, the Bible ceases to be a meaningful norm and guide for faith and practice.

For many churches, however, the danger is on the other side. They inherit church traditions and past conceptions of a Christian worldview and defend them tooth and nail. Indeed, they usually know where to find a Bible verse to prove that their way of thinking is the only Christian option. Viewpoints are labeled as unquestionable biblical truth when in fact they are often no more than inherited traditions or, at most, applications of biblical texts that once made sense in a quite different context.

Whichever of these pitfalls we fall into—uncritically abandoning Christian tradition or uncritically holding on to it—we are guilty of abandoning the Bible as the guide for faith and practice.

There must be a middle way, a way that faithfully practices the principle that Paul taught: "Test everything; hold fast to what is good" (1 Thessalonians 5:21). Neither current cultural trends nor old faith traditions can serve as faithful guides. We need to learn what it means for the Bible to serve as our norm, and we need to learn to interpret the Bible appropriately so that it can indeed provide the guidance we seek and need.

Sola Scriptura—Really?

The middle way is perhaps the hardest way. It requires us to keep the Scriptures central and simultaneously to take a critical stance toward both our culture and our church traditions. That is no small challenge, but it is necessary. After all, "the Scriptures alone" does not answer our questions. In fact the Scriptures alone do nothing at all. They sit quietly, closed and waiting for us to examine, interpret, and apply them. No matter what we mean by "the Scriptures alone," we cannot claim that the Scriptures somehow interpret themselves without our involvement.

The guidance we seek is indeed to be found there, but it must be sought and recognized. Moreover, to find guidance in Scripture we need more than knowledge of the Bible's contents, more than exhaustive concordances and Bible dictionaries, and more than a great reverence for the written Word of God. We need appropriate strategies for finding guidance within the pages of Scripture. And we need hearts that are ready to accept what

Scripture teaches, no matter which aspects of our church tradition, culture, or personal lifestyle choices the Bible may call into
question.

What sometimes troubles us, perhaps even discourages us,
is that many Christians diligently aim to find in Scripture the
guidance they need, but then discover that they are in serious
disagreement with others seeking just as diligently for the meaning of the texts.

Nothing But Timeless Truths?

As much as we might wish it to be otherwise, the Bible is simply *not* a book that speaks only timeless truths designed to say the
same thing to every person in every period and in every culture.
The Bible is very much a historical book. It allows us to observe
how God spoke in the past to various people and in various situations. If God is going to use these biblical texts to speak to us
today, in our circumstances, it will often be an indirect word. *We*
will hear God if we are attentive to how *others* heard God. The
challenge is to listen carefully to how God spoke to others in the
past, so that we might discern how God may wish to use the same
texts to speak to us today. But God may not say the same thing
to us today that God said to them in their day.

Take the promises of Scripture as an example. Most of them
are specifically intended as promises to concrete persons in equally concrete historical situations. They are normally not intended
for us to claim as our own. I know that we are often counseled
otherwise: "Just hear and claim the promises for yourselves.
When the Bible makes a promise, God is speaking directly to
us!" Really? That sounds to me like a surefire recipe for unend-
ing disappointment (when claimed promises go unfulfilled) or
for inconsistent and illogical interpretations (as we twist and turn
texts into something we can claim for ourselves).

For example, God promised Abraham and Sarah that they
would have a son in their old age. Indeed, he promised Zechariah

and Elizabeth the very same joy. Yet there would no doubt be numerous couples sorely disappointed if they were to claim that promise as though God were guaranteeing them the same blessing. Are my wife and I expected to claim this promise for ourselves as well? Should we still do so when we are in our eighties and nineties? Should everyone claim the promise whether they are married or not? If they did, would God be obligated to honor their expectations? Clearly not. The promise of bearing a son in old age was a specific promise given to specific people. It was never intended to be claimed by every Bible reader.

A second example: when Jesus said, "Do not worry beforehand about what you are to say; but say whatever is given you at that time, for it is not you who speak, but the Holy Spirit" (Mark 13:11), he certainly did not mean that those who preach the Word should depend on nothing but the spontaneous leading of the Spirit and therefore not prepare their sermons in advance. He was speaking specifically to apostles who would be dragged into court and would not have any time to prepare their defense speeches. I think that is obvious to most people. Yet it is astonishing how often well-meaning people assume that if we want to be true to the Scriptures then we must be of the opinion that everything contained in the Scriptures applies equally and directly to all readers in every situation. Many want to believe that nothing in Scripture is situation specific or time conditioned. They want everything to be timeless and universal. Some even believe that in order for the Scriptures to speak with authority, the message of Scripture and all its parts *must* be timeless and universal.

But the fact is, many parts of the Scriptures would produce nothing but nonsense if we forced them to apply to everyone equally and in all situations. And our grand attempts to preserve the authority of Scripture end up backfiring as we do all sorts of mental gymnastics, trying to figure out the interpretation of each text that is required for it to be something we can universalize.

The problem I have attempted to illustrate using the Bible's promises is just as easily demonstrated if we think of the Bible's commands and prohibitions. When Jesus instructed the apostles, "Take nothing for your journey, no staff, nor bag, nor bread, nor money—not even an extra tunic" (Luke 9:3), he intended those instructions to apply to his disciples on their upcoming missionary journey, not to all people, at all times, on whatever journeys they are planning to take.

Nevertheless, it is also true that there are timeless promises in Scripture; there are instructions that apply to all people at all times; there are prohibitions that everyone is expected to observe. It won't do to take Jesus' word in Mark 11:25, "Whenever you stand praying, forgive, if you have anything against anyone; so that your Father in heaven may also forgive you your trespasses," and get ourselves off the hook by saying, "That probably applies to other people in other situations, not to me in mine." We cannot quote Paul's word in Ephesians 5:1-2, "Therefore be imitators of God, as beloved children, and live in love, as Christ loved us," and then follow it up with, "But the text does not apply to me."

Turning our attention back to the promises of Scripture, what about this promise in Joshua 1:5-6: "I will be with you; I will not fail you or forsake you. Be strong and courageous"? Does it apply to me as well? Of course it does. But the other half of Joshua 1:6 clearly does *not* apply to me: "For you shall put this people in possession of the land that I swore to their ancestors to give them." Here God is specifically addressing Joshua about the possession of the Promised Land *back then*.

But precisely here we recognize the difficulties that arise. How do we know when a word of Scripture directly applies to us and when it does not? How do we know when the great promises recorded in Scripture are meant for us to claim for ourselves and when they were never intended to be taken that way? How do we know whether God is speaking *to us* when Mark 10:21 says, "Sell what you own, and give the money to the poor" or whether that was meant only for the so-called rich young ruler? How do we know whether speaking in tongues is or is not intended as a gift for use in the church today? How do we know whether women should wear head coverings when they pray in worship gatherings or whether the instructions Paul gave the church applied only to the situation at hand and only to the culture of the day? How do we know which, if any, of the biblical restrictions placed on women in church ministry still apply to the western church in the twenty-first century?

The conviction, pious as it sounds, that everything is to be applied literally—all promises are to be claimed, all commands to be followed, all prohibitions observed by all people and at all times—in fact helps us far less than we would hope when trying to find appropriate applications of biblical teaching. The problem is that this conviction simply cannot be consistently practiced. And when we claim this principle but practice it inconsistently, it should not surprise us that we have a hard time finding consensus on what is to be believed and practiced, even among those who claim to live by this conviction. Many claim to believe that everything in the Bible is to be interpreted and applied literally. However, I have never met a person who came even remotely close to living consistent with this principle. Everyone abandons such a principle when it mandates beliefs and practices that are simply impossible and often ridiculous. And it is good that they abandon their principle, at least at times, for the principle itself is far from adequate in guiding our attempts to understand and apply the Bible's teaching.

The simple rules, the pious sounding claims, and the clear guidelines all seem attractive and helpful in theory, but they simply do not lead to the goal. They don't work well when we try to implement them, and they stand in tension with what the Bible is. The Bible is a collection of books, letters, and documents of various sorts written in specific concrete historical situations. If we want to hear God's voice through these, we need to do more than simply read it directly off the page, regardless of who wrote it, to whom, and why.

In the end, the "simple clear guidelines" actually only *seem* simple. When those who profess to adopt these guidelines abandon them because they simply don't work, we have a recipe for disaster. Seeking consensus on what the Bible teaches is made more difficult, not easier. The temptation is strong to bend and twist the Bible to make it say whatever I want to believe rather than honestly seeking guidance from the Scriptures as our norm for faith and life.

My goal in what follows is to present a series of considerations designed to help us think in a more nuanced way about the nature and the function of the Bible. I hope that when we do so, we will also be able to develop better strategies for hearing Scripture, both with sensitive ears and with obedient hearts.

A 'People of the Book'—Four Aspects

Christians often think of themselves as "people of the book." But does that necessarily mean that we are expected to apply literally everything we find in the Bible? I don't think so. Rather, to be people of the book means our approach to Scripture is characterized as follows:

First, we put our trust in God's Word. When critical Bible scholars claim to know better than the authors of the texts what "really happened" in the biblical stories, when they presume to rewrite biblical history from their privileged position as "people who know" at the expense of authors who were much closer to the events described and inspired by God to write about them, we respond with a resounding no. The scientists change their theories every few years anyway. The Bible remains a reliable guide.

Second, we seek in Scripture "the way, and the truth, and the life," and we find Jesus himself proclaimed there. Jesus said to some of those rejecting him: "You search the scriptures because you think that in them you have eternal life; and it is they that testify on my behalf. Yet you refuse to come to me to have life" (John 5:39-40). If the book itself takes center stage, we are not truly a people of the book, for we will have adopted a different center than that spoken by the Scriptures themselves. To be a people of the book is to put Christ at the center.

Third, we examine all claims in the light of the Scriptures. If someone claims to have come to a new insight concerning God or God's truth, we examine that claim in the light of the Scriptures. If someone claims the right to abandon a long-standing tradition of the church, we examine the Scriptures to see whether they allow for the new possibility; we look in the Scriptures to see whether the proposed new direction is a valid application of biblical teaching. If someone claims to have heard a word from the Lord, whether it came in private Bible reading, in prayer, or through a prophetic word, we go to the Bible and test it in the light of revealed truth. Does it correspond to what the Bible teaches? And of course we not only examine the claims of others in the light of Scripture but also our own claims. After all, we are not a people of the book if we use the Bible only to find support for our own convictions. When the Bible no longer has the power (or our permission) to call into question our own opinions, we have stripped it of its authority altogether.

Fourth, we consider to be most important that which the Bible considers most important. So often we fight about secondary issues and ignore the most important emphases of Scripture. Jesus regularly criticized those who "tithe mint, dill, and cumin, and have neglected the weightier matters of the law: justice and mercy and faith" (Matthew 23:23). Perhaps if Jesus had addressed us he might have criticized our overly scrupulous prooftexting to defend our long-cherished beliefs about the Bible's teaching while neglecting the weightier matter of working toward unity and mutual acceptance in the church—even with those who interpret texts differently.

Attending to Scripture—Four Goals

It is clear that we all want to find guidelines for Christian living within the Scriptures. Unfortunately it is far less clear how that works. I want to share some of my personal priorities when attending to the Scriptures.

First, I want to allow individual texts to speak to me rather than merely using those texts to support a theory or bolster a conviction of mine. I have become increasingly convinced that God's Spirit shapes us when we allow texts of Scripture to work in us, that is, we hear the Word, we seek understanding, we allow ourselves to be spoken to, challenged, inspired, and formed. The foremost goal is not to extract from the text some hidden "answer" to questions that we bring with us. Our stance is rather that of a listener. We want to internalize the challenges and invitations of the text. Walter Brueggemann speaks of texts "funding the imagination."[1] That is the goal. We are not trying to find the one right answer to an ethical question or the one right doctrinal statement to resolve a theological issue. We are not looking for the missing puzzle piece that completes the picture or for the one elusive clue that harmonizes this text with the rest of the Bible. We are sitting under the Word and listening to it.

Second, I search the Scriptures not only for answers but also for appropriate ways of seeking answers. We have plenty of questions: Is divorce allowed? Is it right for a Christian to fight in the military? Is it a sin to disobey a traffic law? Is it always a sin to have an abortion? Would it be wrong to invest my money in this way? Yet often the Scriptures give us something other than clear answers. Instead, they give us guidance that enables us to deal with our questions honestly and with integrity. They provide us with principles that we need to take seriously if we are looking for concrete help. They teach us how to listen to God's Spirit, how to make wise decisions as a community, and how to work toward a consensus that God can support. Sometimes we even find clear answers—but only sometimes.

Third, I want to be sensitive to God's plans and purposes, not just assemble a list of rules and regulations. In Mark 10:3, Jesus responds to a question from the Pharisees with a question: "What did Moses command you?" As the Pharisees quote a passage in Deuteronomy, Jesus interrupts them and essentially tells them, "Wrong text!" He knew they were quoting a text that provided no help in determining God's larger intentions. If we try to determine God's will but in the process quote the "wrong" texts, our findings will not be biblical, even if we can cite chapter and verse. Some people wish that at the end of every Bible study we could establish a clear set of biblical guidelines, rules, and regulations regarding the topic at hand. Others fear the legalism that could easily result from such an approach. If we fix our eyes on God's larger purposes rather than only on the applicable rules, we often find a middle way between stifling legalism and unbridled freedom.

Fourth, I want to pay careful attention to diversity, both in the Bible and in life. The Bible has a variety of perspectives on issues precisely because life throws up so many different kinds of situations. God is faithful and true, loving and generous to all. But God often acts differently in response to varying situations. And in this, God is a model for us. The people we meet are not "cases." They are unique individuals whose experiences are never exactly the same as the experiences of others. The Bible often helps us to see things from more than one perspective, which in turn equips us to supportively help others as they encounter a variety of unique life situations. Each person is called to respond to Jesus, to discover what discipleship means, to act responsibly, and to experience God's guidance. But what that looks like will vary from person to person, from situation to situation. We err when we seek to eliminate the diversity we encounter in Scripture. Instead, we should value Scripture's diversity, trusting God's Spirit to lead us as we discern which text provides the guidance we need in the situations with which we are confronted. We cannot live without any guidelines, but neither can we put people in boxes and expect identical behavior from everyone; nor can we apply rules without concern for the actual circumstances of the people involved. That is not the biblical way or the way of Jesus.

The Roles of Scripture—Four Metaphors

I find various metaphors helpful for describing how the Scriptures actually "function." The truth is that the Scriptures often function on more than one level, and not all texts do so in the same way.

The Bible as window. The Bible often serves to reveal to us what God did in history. It reveals how God was active, how God created a believing community, and how God was at work in the world. When we observe all this, we are looking *through* the text to what lies *behind* it. The text functions like a window into an earlier time. As we look through the window, we can observe how people lived, how God interacted with them, and how Jesus ministered to people. We see how the Holy Spirit led the early church, how Paul planted churches, and much more. Often a glimpse of what happened then sensitizes us to what God is doing today. The lessons God's people learned back then become lessons we learn today. Thus the Bible becomes a window into God's ways with humankind, and the history of God's people becomes our history as well.

The Bible as portrait gallery. The Bible shows us a multitude of positive and negative models. The biblical characters are not only historical persons; they are also literary characters. Sometimes we do not look through the Bible and find something historical behind it, but rather we look *into* the Bible and find something *within* the text itself. We discover characters of all sorts, good and bad, presented to us by the biblical writers. Which are there to instruct and inspire us? Which are there to warn us? As we meet each character, we wonder which characteristics and actions should be imitated and which are merely aspects of that character's culture. These are the questions that arise when the Bible functions as a portrait gallery. There is much to learn from the characters we meet there and much to learn from the authors who painted these portraits in such vibrant colors.

The Bible as mirror. The Bible shows me what I am like. In fact, quite often the historical and the literary characters are not central to the Bible's revelation. I am. The Bible helps me to recognize myself in its pages. I see myself there: "Yes, that is exactly what I am like." "I need that as well." "I have the very same question." And thus the Bible becomes a *mirror*. If I will let it happen, the Bible will *read me*. It will clarify my inner needs, my attitudes, and my hidden desires. When these are illuminated, God ministers to me by meeting my needs, shaping my attitudes, and fulfilling my desires.

The Bible as glasses. The Bible enables me to see more clearly. I learn to see not only the characters, not only myself, but everything else in a new way. I learn to see the world with God's eyes and to see God with new eyes of faith. Put another way, the Bible sometimes performs its desired role not by showing me something I had never seen before but by enabling me to see things I have always seen, but to see them from God's perspective. To be immersed in the Scriptures is to put on a new pair of glasses. If I can see myself, the world, and life itself from God's perspective, that is sometimes enough to make clear what God is asking me to do and be.

From Texts to Life—Four Tasks

In his very helpful book on Bible interpretation, *The Moral Vision of the New Testament*, Richard Hays proposes four tasks, or steps, that can help us think biblically when we seek appropriate ethical guidance and Christian standards.

First, the descriptive task. What do the texts say? What is the correct way to interpret them? What diversity is there in the Bible on the topic at hand? What are the common themes?

Second, the synthetic task. How do the individual texts on a theme fit into the witness of the whole Bible on that topic? How do various helpful "lenses" (that is, theological perspectives) assist us in seeing the bigger picture? (For Hays, the best lenses through which to view the message of the Bible as a whole are "community," "cross," and "new creation.")

Third, the hermeneutical task. What exactly does the Bible offer on the given topic? Does it provide rules to live by? Principles to guide our thinking? Examples and models to encourage, instruct, and warn us? Insights that help shape a Christian worldview? As we receive what Scripture offers, what roles are played by the traditions we have inherited, our past experience, the experiences of others, and human reason?

Finally, the pragmatic task. How are we to apply the Bible's message? What does it mean to live faithfully in this world? In what ways do we stand out as a community of contrast to the ways of the world? How do we concretely practice the teaching of Scripture in the realities of life?

Naturally we do not have to follow precisely the steps that Hays outlines in order to gain guidance from Scripture. Nevertheless his suggestions and examples are instructive if we want the Bible to be a normative guide for faith and life.

Exegesis and Hermeneutics

Many Bible interpreters (for example, Gordon Fee and Douglas Stuart in *How to Read the Bible for All Its Worth*) propose that we make a clear separation between exegesis (which approximately corresponds to the first two of Hays's tasks) and hermeneutics (the last two of his tasks). I find it helpful to carefully distinguish between these two, though admittedly they cannot and should not be completely separated. If we want to be guided by Scripture we first need to ask what the text says (exegesis) and then examine what is involved in appropriately applying the message of the text (hermeneutics). When we exegete the text, we are attempting to hear what God said through the original author to the original readers. When we practice hermeneutics, we are seeking to hear God's message to us in our situation through the ancient texts.

Tools that help us with exegesis are good translations (they actually do a lot of the exegetical work for us), some information about the circumstances in which the texts were written, a general knowledge of the Bible and its message, and an understanding of the primary message of the book we are examining. These tools will help us to read the texts as the first readers did, and thus in the way the author originally intended. Of course, our exegesis is never guaranteed to be correct. We depend on God's Spirit to help us, but even so our knowledge is always imperfect. It is the Bible, not our attempts to understand it, that merits the term *infallible*. We learn to listen to each other, to benefit from the insights of Bible interpreters and commentary writers, and thus to pursue the goal of "hearing Scripture." But the results of all this exegetical work are still just the first step. We have attempted to hear what the texts say, but we have not yet begun the second step. The results of our exegesis do not automatically provide us with insight as to what we are to do with what we have understood. For that we need to take the second step.

An attempt to understand 1 Corinthians 11 provides a good example. Our goal is to correctly discern what Paul was telling the Corinthians in this chapter. Most interpreters are persuaded that Paul was teaching the Corinthians that when they prayed or prophesied in a Christian gathering, the women should have long hair and a head covering, while the men should have short hair and no head covering. As part of our exegesis, we examine this conclusion (for there are indeed other options!). Have we correctly heard Paul?

But even when we have completed our exegetical work, we are far from finished. Those who claim that a literal application of all texts is the only way to be faithful to Scripture might think we are done, but we have already seen that this claim is both inappropriate and impossible to follow through on. What is needed is the second step. We have heard Paul speak to the Corinthians. But we must now ask, "What is God saying to us through the word that Paul spoke to the Corinthians?" That is the question of application, of hermeneutics, and to answer that question we need to consider a number of valid approaches.

How Does the Textual Message Address Us?—Four Approaches

Without making it more complicated than necessary, I would like to describe four different approaches to moving from the original message of the texts to an appropriate application of these messages in another time and place.

1. Applying the text directly. We hear what the text said back then and allow the same message to directly address us today. That is, the commands obligate us to obey, the prohibitions name things we too must avoid, the promises are there for us to claim for ourselves, and so forth.
2. Applying the text's principle(s) in new ways. Here we listen to the text, discern which principles are being taught or applied, and then find appropriate, though often quite different, ways of applying those principles to a new situation.
3. Moving into the world of the text. Here the goal is not to bring the text's message to us, but rather to transport ourselves into the world of the text, allowing ourselves then to be guided by what the text is teaching.
4. Listening to the voice of the Spirit. Here we take the posture of a discerning listener, even when we cannot provide objective proofs that what we have discerned is logically derived from rational exegetical and hermeneutical work.

I would like to examine these four approaches more fully and suggest ways of evaluating their contribution to the task of understanding and applying Scripture, discerning God's will for us personally and corporately, and working toward consensus in the Christian community.

Applying the text directly. I have already addressed this approach. In theory it sounds so "biblical," "reliable," "simple and safe." Just do what the text says! If not *always*, at least that should be the default position. Unfortunately this approach is not as easy or as appropriate as it sounds. Though there are many texts for which a literal and direct application is both possible and desirable, there are literally hundreds of situations in which that is not the case. If our only option is to "apply literally," we will quickly discover that we need to excise from our Bible huge parts of the Old Testament. Otherwise we would find ourselves in a situation in which selling our daughters into slavery would be allowed, in which we would be required to stone people who do not keep the Sabbath, and in which it would be forbidden to cut the edges of our beards. It would mean we would have to avoid all clothing made of two kinds of thread (for example, cotton and polyester), that farmers could not sow two kinds of seed in the same field, and so on. In fact, we would also have significant difficulty practicing this approach with a large number of New Testament texts.

We know that the New Testament expressly releases us from some of the obligations that applied in Old Testament times (for example, food laws and regulations concerning animal sacrifices). But even so we are left with numerous situations in which no New Testament texts guide us in discerning the appropriate application of Old Testament prohibitions and commands. If we were to assume that wherever there is any doubt, we are obligated to apply the text directly to our situation, we would have to put a huge question mark over hundreds of things that average Christians take for granted, or else cut out huge parts of the Old Testament (and not a little of the New as well!). Otherwise (and in my opinion this is a better alternative) we would have to look for other approaches to Scripture to help us in places where the direct-application approach is either impossible or probably not what God expects of us.

Applying the text's principle(s) in new ways. Often a direct application is not possible or, even if possible, not appropriate. Often a direct application is not the goal of the text. In many such situations we take the text seriously and follow its guidance by identifying the principle that lies behind the direct teaching of the text and then applying this principle in new and appropriate ways in our very different situation. Let me illustrate.

If we truly believed we were required to obey every command we found in the Bible, we would have a great deal of difficulty with this text: "Get up, take the child and his mother, and flee to Egypt, and remain there until I tell you" (Matthew 2:13). Am I really supposed to imagine that I am being addressed by this text? Should I go book a flight to Cairo? Which of my children should I take with me? Even if I could figure out how to obey this command literally, what about all those who have no wife or no child? How will they obey the command recorded in this text? They cannot, neither do they need to. The text reports what an angel told Joseph in a dream when the baby Jesus' life was threatened, not what God is saying to everyone who reads the text. But might we discern principles in the text that do apply to us? Certainly.

An example of such a principle might be this: It pays to listen for God's guidance; God might want to warn us and thus protect us from imminent danger. Or perhaps we might uncover the principle that God's plan of salvation will be brought to completion, for God is a faithful God. Human attempts to thwart God's plans will not succeed. The principles taught by a text can be identified and applied even when no direct application is possible or desired.

Here is a second example. A great deal that Paul writes to his young co-worker Timothy applies directly to us. He writes, "Hold to the standard of sound teaching that you have heard from me, in the faith and love that are in Christ Jesus. Guard the good treasure entrusted to you, with the help of the Holy Spirit living in us. . . . Be strong in the grace that is in Christ Jesus" (2 Timothy 1:13-14; 2:1). The apostle might well have been speaking directly to me. But I feel less directly addressed when Paul writes later in his letter, "Bring the cloak that I left with Carpus at Troas, also the books, and above all the parchments" (4:13). Even if I could undertake a pilgrimage to Troas, Paul's coat and books (and for that matter Carpus) would no longer be there, nor does Paul need them anymore. Does that mean that this text has lost its relevance or that we can simply ignore it? Not at all. We can continue to learn from a text like this. It teaches, for example, that it is a Christian virtue to help each other in times of need and therefore completely appropriate also to ask for needed help. God is concerned not only for spiritual matters but also for our physical well-being and the stimulation of our minds.

Of course, none of us would ever have imagined we were obligated by the Scriptures to make a trip to Egypt or to Troas. But why then do so many Christians respond in other situations by saying, "Don't ask about the historical situation of a text; just listen to it and do what it says, otherwise you are not being faithful to Scripture"? It's one thing to say that, but I will start taking them seriously when I see that they have booked their flights to Egypt and to Troas. The fact is that virtually every text in the Bible is linked to a particular historical circumstance. Taking that into consideration is not avoiding the message of Scripture or adopting a situational ethic. It is in fact our best chance of truly hearing Scripture as it was intended to be heard. This does not mean that an appropriate application of a text's principle will always be completely different from the application written into the historical text. Often they will be similar, sometimes identical. But we still have to question what lies behind the concrete instructions in a text. What does that text have to say to a situation that is different from the original one?

Though it may not always be easy to discern the principle being illustrated or taught in a text, it is always worth the effort of attempting to discern it. Doing so will often lead us to the goal of the text. For this reason, this second approach to Scripture is often sufficient to determine an appropriate application. Nevertheless, I have three small words of caution:

First, we must guard against examining the text, discerning the principle, *and then discarding the text.* The principles we discern are intended to help us discover suitable applications. They are not intended to become substitutes for the text. God gave us *texts.* The principles we claim to discover must be continually reevaluated in the light of the texts themselves. In fact, when our situation changes, we might well find ourselves discovering new principles in the same texts we once thought we fully understood.

Second, we must admit that our search for principles can be very subjective. The truth is that we will often find in a text precisely those principles we need in order to support our previously held opinions or justify our lifestyles. If a text is no longer permitted to call into question our conclusions or our behavior, the Bible is no longer an authority over us, no matter how strongly we may affirm that it is.

Third, though the search for principles is important, it does not guarantee consensus. Christians often disagree about what the Bible teaches on a given topic. But that is not always the result of interpreting the words and the sentences differently. In fact we might well agree on what an author was saying to the original readers. Our exegesis might be identical. Still we disagree on the teaching of Scripture. Why? Because we discern different principles in the texts.

With some texts, this is not likely to happen. For example, it is not hard to discover the principles in a text like Romans 14:13-23. Paul is instructing the Roman Christians how to deal with their disagreements over whether Christians may eat "unclean" food. He urges them to be sensitive to the possible negative impact of their actions on other Christians. If the full exercise of their freedom causes other believers to stumble, they should be willing to restrict their freedoms for the sake of others. At the same time he teaches that Christians should follow their own convictions and not stand in judgment over each other. Principles like these can certainly be applied in a variety of other situations.

But what is the principle behind Paul's counsel to the Corinthians that women should wear head coverings and that men and women should have different lengths of hair (see 1 Corinthians 11:2-16)? Here are some possibilities:

1. The outward appearance of Christians should not violate the norms of a given culture, so that people do not take offense at the gospel for the wrong reasons.
2. Characteristic differences in appearance between men and women should be carefully maintained in order to symbolize the fact that the man is the head of the woman.
3. It is appropriate for women to practice precisely the same spiritual gifts and ministries as men, as long as they do not attempt, by their appearance, to deny their womanhood.

If we discover mutually contradictory principles in a given text, it should not surprise us to discover that this second approach is not a surefire secret recipe for consensus in the Christian community. It is a helpful approach. But it provides no guarantee that all our problems related to the application of Scripture will be solved.

Moving into the world of the text. Here I want to try to reformulate the second approach (discerning principles), not because it necessarily makes things easier, but because it seems to take more seriously the nature of Scripture. Some people read the Bible as though it were nothing but a book of hidden principles, hidden theological claims, hidden ethical teachings. They assume that our assignment is to find all these hidden lessons and to reorganize them, collecting together all the lessons on similar themes. Out of these collections, we are to derive our ethics, write our theology, and offer our books of practical advice for the church. What emerges is a normative systematic theology or a code of ethics or a manual for church organization, or whatever. And if we were completely honest, we would have to admit that these often play a more significant role in our lives than the texts from which we extracted our hidden principles.

But the Bible is not merely a preparatory stage in the development of clever theology. In fact, it is not even first and foremost a theology book itself. The Bible is a story, a grand story consisting of many sub-stories. The Bible is the story of God's dealings with humanity.

We are a part of this story. Of course, the Scriptures do contain doctrinal statements and ethical instructions and promises. But these are all embedded in a story. Our goal is not merely to extract principles from the texts. Rather it is to follow the texts' invitation to enter into them, to be immersed in the story they tell, to become participants. When we enter the story, we learn from and alongside all those others who have participated in the story—the prophets, the men and women who followed Jesus, the early missionaries, the Corinthian Christians, and so on. Along with them we learn what God is like, how God deals with people, how God leads, what it means to follow Jesus. In other words, we are not extracting principles out of the texts; we are entering into the texts.

Yet the difference between these two approaches is not as large as it might seem. In this approach we still need to build a bridge connecting the world of the text to our own world. We cross this bridge in one direction when we enter the world of the text; we cross it again in the other, taking what we have learned and bringing it with us back into our own world. After all, our task is not to live out the lessons of Scripture in the *ancient* world, but in *our* world. When we cross the bridge from the ancient world back into ours, we are not doing anything very different from those practicing the second approach, discovering the appropriate principles and reapplying them in a new context. But at least with this present approach we are treating the Bible as a story and not as a book of hidden doctrines and hidden ethical guidelines. That is a step forward, even if it does not automatically make the matter of application simpler.

Listening to the voice of the Spirit. This is my suggested fourth approach. It sounds very spiritual. Who could possibly say anything against it? Before I do in fact say something against it, let me assert something very clearly: I believe that the Holy Spirit does speak to us when we read and study the Scriptures. Indeed, the Spirit sometimes throws our preconceived ideas completely overboard, showing us things in Scripture that we never thought we would discover there, things that we did not even *want* to find there.

Still, not everything that "occurs to us" when we read the Bible is a direct communication from the Spirit of God. Even things that occur to us when we are putting our best efforts into listening for God's voice are not necessarily revelation from God. I would go so far as to say that we ought to have a fairly healthy skepticism about the private revelations we think we are receiving, especially when others around us cannot confirm those insights. The church needs to discern carefully whether people claiming such revelations are truly hearing directly from God's Spirit.

In our quiet times with God, we can indeed expect to meet God and to hear God's voice. I don't want to cast any doubt on that. But when people claim God has directly told them what a passage of Scripture means, how it should be applied, what the rest of us should believe and practice, then I want to be very cautious. Not because things like that don't happen, but because they need to be confirmed.

The early church was indeed able to say, "It has seemed good to the Holy Spirit and to us" (Acts 15:28). But that was after the gathered community was able to reach a consensus, which is very different from one Bible reader saying, "It seems good to the Holy Spirit and to me."

I suspect that what we sometimes call "the voice of God" or "the leading of the Holy Spirit" is more likely a mixture of what God is indeed saying, our inherited traditions, our personal preferences, our wishes, and insights we think we have gained from the texts but have sometimes read into the texts. My personal convictions—no matter how sure I am that God was speaking—are seldom a reliable guide on their own.

Nevertheless, I do not believe our insights are merely distractions to be ignored. Even if we give a new label to these insights, even if we stop calling them "the voice of the Holy Spirit" and instead call them no more than impressions or "gut feelings," they nevertheless can play a helpful role in learning to understand and apply biblical texts. Everyone has gut feelings about certain texts, and not everyone can explain exactly why they are convinced that one interpretation of the Bible on a given topic or in a given text is preferable to another.

Where do these gut feelings come from? Well, as already suggested, they might well come from various factors working together—tradition, the insights from Scripture, convictions about what God is like, our sense of what is most important in the Bible, our beliefs about the topics addressed in a text, our logical thinking, *and* the leading of the Spirit, which we so much want to experience. As mixed as these gut feelings may be, they can protect us from serious error. When we look closely at what has counted as "biblical exegesis" throughout church history—when we note what impossible strategies have been used, what sorts of allegorical playing with the texts has been tolerated and even valued—we cannot help but be horrified. At times every text was thought to have four different levels of meaning and those thus convinced somehow found all four, whatever they had to do to fabricate them. Nevertheless, even these Bible interpreters (if we can use the expression loosely) often stayed closer to the core teaching of Scripture than a host of others whose methods were more defensible and whose logic was more solid, but their hearts were not in close contact with God, the church, and the claims of Scripture on their lives.

Well-considered and carefully practiced interpretive methods provide no guarantee of reliable exegesis and hermeneutics. The gut feeling of a sincere follower of Jesus seeking truth through the pages of Scripture is often more reliable than the logical thinking of many theologians.

Let me say this still more provocatively. Imagine I have two people in front of me. One is a young theologian, a recent graduate from seminary, well equipped with Bible knowledge, with a carefully worked-out systematic theology, even with a working knowledge of the original biblical languages. Moreover, our imaginary student is clever, can think logically, and can argue persuasively. The other person is over eighty and has never been to seminary or Bible school. In fact, he never even finished high school. He has never read a theology book, but he has had a lifetime relationship with Jesus and the church. He loves the Bible dearly and reads it daily.

So now the church is struggling to reach consensus on a controversial issue. What does the Bible teach? Both of our imaginary believers hold strong convictions. The young theologian can argue his case with persuasive words and powerful logic. The older member is no match in terms of logic and persuasion, but he's very uneasy about the direction the young theologian wants the church to go.

Whose viewpoint should the church take more carefully into consideration? My response: the church should pay at least as close attention to the gut feeling of the elderly Jesus-follower as to the clever arguments of the seminary graduate—maybe even more! Of course, they need one another, and the church needs them both. But it would be a grave error if the intuitive gut feeling did not count because it could not be logically defended. God's Spirit brings into being such gut feelings at least as often as God's Spirit produces clever theological arguments.

Conclusion

I have described and evaluated four different approaches to applying Scripture: we apply directly, we apply principles, we move into the text, and we listen to God's Spirit. Which is the *right* approach? All of them are. All of them can be appropriate, depending on the situation and the text and the topic. Each approach can correct the weaknesses of the others. We are better off if we take all four into consideration than if we pick our favorite and try to make it answer all our questions.

It may well be more difficult to reach a consensus if one person favors the first approach, another the second, and still others the third or the fourth. But my view is the decisions we make will far more likely be within appropriate biblical boundaries if we permit this diversity than if we recognize only one of these options and disallow the other three. This of course assumes that each person in the community is willing to listen sympathetically to the viewpoints of the others and that each person is willing to join a growing consensus, even if that consensus moves in a direction that some individuals do not see as the best possible choice. In the church we must learn to make decisions together that not everyone considers the correct ones. When we do, we must not label these decisions "God's perfect will" or "the true biblical teaching." Rather, we call our decisions the best we could do under the circumstances. We reached them through careful attention to what the Scriptures say and equally careful attention to what kind of application is appropriate for our situation.

May God give us great patience with one another, much joy in studying the Scriptures, and an extra measure of eagerness to find common convictions in our life together. When we are able to make good decisions, we celebrate! And ten years later, at the very latest, we open up all the same questions again and ask, "Do we still see it that way? Have we gained new insights as to what the biblical texts say? Has our situation changed sufficiently that the unchanging Word of God should be applied in a new way today?"

Discussion Questions

1. How can the Bible most effectively speak into our lives?

2. Which of the claims presented here, either about the Bible itself or about the best strategies for interpreting and applying it, seem to you to be most helpful? Which are you skeptical of?

3. How have you experienced the Holy Spirit helping and guiding your congregation as you have sought guidance from the Scriptures?

For Further Reading

Fee, Gordon, and Douglas Stuart. *How to Read the Bible for All Its Worth: A Guide to Understanding the Bible*. Grand Rapids, MI: Zondervan, 2003.

Hays, Richard. *The Moral Vision of the New Testament*. San Francisco: Harper, 1996.

Tate, Randolph. *Biblical Interpretation: An Integrated Approach*. Peabody, MA: Hendrickson, 1997.

Virkler, Henry A. and Karelynne Gerber Ayayo. *Hermeneutics: Principles and Processes of Biblical Interpretation*. Grand Rapids, MI: Baker, 2007.

2

Matthew 18:

Reconciliation and Mutual Accountability

In Matthew 18, Jesus portrays the discipleship community. We learn what it means for him to be in our midst and for reconciliation and mutual accountability to characterize our common life.

We live in a pluralistic world. There was a time when western society was at least nominally Christian and there was general agreement regarding questions of right and wrong. Ethical convictions today are more often personal, more like norms and guidelines, rather than "societal standards." And our personal convictions vary greatly. What are typical responses to the changed situation? Here are some examples:

> I am responsible to no one but myself. I seek my own ethical guidelines. As long as I don't hurt other people, I can do whatever I personally believe is right. (This is a typical viewpoint representing the spirit of our individualistic age.)

> I have the Bible and I have a conscience. I can decide for myself what I believe is right and wrong. (This is the typical Christian viewpoint in our individualistic age.)

I just look for an authority I can trust—my pastor, a Christian writer, or a radio preacher—and that person tells me what the Bible says is right or wrong. (This is a typical evangelical reaction to our society's individualism and to the relativism it often breeds.)

We are in mutually accountable fellowship. I will be present with you and help you to seek ethical guidelines as a community. You will bind and loose each other in my name. (This is how Jesus responds to our individualistic age.)

Martin Luther defined the church as the place where the Word of God is rightly preached and the sacraments of the church are rightly administered. Such a definition of the church provides little motivation to become a responsible community in which members are mutually accountable to one another. The radical reformers of the era, such as Conrad Grebel and Michael Sattler, defined the church quite differently: the church was the place where people freely commit themselves to become disciples of Jesus and freely commit themselves to their brothers and sisters in a discerning community. Such an understanding of the church emphasizes mutual responsibility and relationships of accountability.

Throughout the centuries the spiritual descendants of these early radical reformers have sought to retain and embody this community-oriented understanding of church—sometimes with success, sometimes with serious failures. At times it has degenerated into one of two extremes. On one side lies the practice of heartless legalistic church discipline. On the other side is an attitude of unbounded tolerance in which everyone can do as they please. Anabaptist and Mennonite churches, which have tried to follow the radical reformation path, have found themselves at different times and in different places at every imaginable point between these extremes.

We have not reached the goal. We have not become the church Jesus intended us to be. But those willing to take courageous steps toward this ideal can receive God's help in becoming what Jesus had in mind.

Matthew 18 provides insights that may help us to become the kind of reconciled and responsible community Jesus intended. Nowhere else in Scripture do we find Jesus describing so clearly his ideal for the church. For this reason the early Anabaptist churches considered this chapter to be of central importance in their understanding of "church." So let's examine the chapter and note its basic convictions, warnings, recommendations, and promises that might help us on the way.

Who Is the Greatest?

> At that time the disciples came to Jesus and asked, "Who is the greatest in the kingdom of heaven?" He called a child, whom he put among them, and said, "Truly, I tell you, unless you change and become like children, you will never enter the kingdom of heaven. Whoever becomes humble like this child is the greatest in the kingdom of heaven. Whoever welcomes one such child in my name welcomes me." (Matthew 18:1-5)

If we want to be the church as Jesus intended it, then everything depends on our approach to God's kingdom, the church, and our relationships with each other. Jesus' disciples imagined that God's kingdom would be something like this: Jesus would become a powerful political ruler in a reconstituted free Israelite state and they, his followers, would be at his side—ministers in his government—sharing his glory and his authority. It was not enough to hold fast to the conviction that all of them would be great rulers in the new kingdom. They also wanted to know who among them would have the *most* power and prestige. That is the background to the disciples' question "Who is the greatest in the kingdom of heaven?" (v. 1).

Jesus' reaction, to paraphrase, is "Careful! With that kind of attitude, you won't even be there with me in God's kingdom!" (Note that Matthew's Gospel often speaks of the "kingdom of heaven," but means the same thing as "kingdom of God.") It was clear to Jesus that the time was ripe for another object lesson. He took a child—small, helpless, neither presumptuous nor audacious, without rights and without power—placed the child in their midst and looked at his followers. No doubt they were somewhat taken aback as Jesus made his three astonishing claims:

- This is what you must be like.
- One like this child is the greatest in God's kingdom.
- If you want to accept me, then accept people like this child.

Do we want to become the kind of committed fellowship in which Jesus truly makes his presence felt? If so, the path begins with a change in our attitudes. We do not seek to increase our power and influence; we do not aim to become great according to the standards of this world. Rather, with childlike trust, we accept an entirely new kind of greatness. The greatness Jesus offers is given to us as a gift, if only we will humble ourselves and receive it and thereby receive Jesus. We do not seek rights and privileges; rather, we invest what we are and what we have in the lives of those who are with us on the journey and who are unable to meet the challenges of the discipleship journey on their own—and that is all of us! That is how Jesus' presence becomes tangible among us.

Be Careful About Yourself and Your Influence

"If any of you put a stumbling block before one of these little ones who believe in me, it would be better for you if a great millstone were fastened around your neck and you were drowned in the depth of the sea. Woe to the world because of stumbling blocks! Occasions for stumbling are bound to come, but woe to the one by whom the stumbling block comes!

"If your hand or your foot causes you to stumble, cut it off and throw it away; it is better for you to enter life maimed or lame than to have two hands or two feet and to be thrown into the eternal fire. And if your eye causes you to stumble, tear it out and throw it away; it is better for you to enter life with one eye than to have two eyes and to be thrown into the hell of fire.

"Take care that you do not despise one of these little ones; for, I tell you, in heaven their angels continually see the face of my Father in heaven." (Matthew 18:6-10)

Jesus has just said that children are models for us (v. 3). Now he adds that we are also models for them (v. 6). We observe them and imitate their childlike attitudes; they watch us and see in our actions what is important on the road of discipleship. What a responsibility rests with us! When we are modeling poor behavior, or when children misunderstand our actions and thus we "put a stumbling block before one of these little ones," then we need to hear Jesus' warning: "It would be better for you if a great millstone were fastened around your neck and you were drowned in the depth of the sea." Jesus often used picture language, made drastic claims, and exaggerated to make his point. His goal, of course, is not to terrify us by making us fear that we might qualify for this inescapable drowning (or something so bad that even this would seem preferable!). Nor should we live anxiously, always insecure about whether we have taken a false step and constantly fearing that God's judgment will rain down on us swiftly. With his hyperbolic statement, Jesus was saying as loudly and clearly as possible, "This is important!"

If we want to make progress in the direction that Christ wants to lead us, we need to pay attention to the consequences of our actions on others. This is the only way we can pursue the supremely important goal of helping the "little ones"—the vulnerable and easily wounded beginners on the road of disciple-ship. Jesus speaks of the drastic measures we should be willing to take: Cut off the hand; hack off the foot; tear out the eye! Again he uses hyperbole. He clearly does not mean it literally; but he does mean it seriously. We are asked to take drastic measures, if necessary, to avoid irresistible temptations ourselves and to keep from putting stumbling blocks in the way of the little ones.

Jesus knows how easily we begin to resent others, particular-ly those whose weakness ends up costing us some of our free-dom. So he says, "Do not despise one of these little ones" (v. 10). On the contrary, Jesus commands us to protect them and help them, just as God does. God even charges the heavenly angels to watch over the vulnerable ones.

In some translations (for example, the King James Version, the New King James Version, and the New American Standard Bible), verse 11 reads, "For the Son of Man has [is] come to save that which was lost." In virtually all other translations this verse is omitted and often a footnote explains that it is not in earlier Bible manuscripts. Very likely it was added later by copyists. Still it is appropriate to this context. If God took such extraordinary measures to bring us onto the right path (sending the Son to seek and save us), we want to make our contribution toward helping others as they walk along this path with us.

Seeking, Finding, Celebrating

> "What do you think? If a shepherd has a hundred sheep, and one of them has gone astray, does he not leave the ninety-nine on the mountains and go in search of the one that went astray? And if he finds it, truly I tell you, he rejoices over it more than over the ninety-nine that never went astray. So it is not the will of your Father in heaven that one of these little ones should be lost." (18:12-14)

Most of us know that Jesus used the parable of the lost sheep to explain to people why he was eating at the same table with tax collectors and sinners. He was *seeking* these people. And having found them, he was *celebrating* with them. But that explanation is found in Luke 15. We should not read that interpretation into *this* text, because here the same parable is used for a very different purpose.

In Matthew the Christian community is the flock. We are the vulnerable sheep. All our attempts to flee temptation, to be the right kinds of models for others, and to help people along the way will never produce the perfect community. They cannot, because the community is made up of fallible people. Some will go astray; they will do something that distances them from the shepherd and his flock. And we ourselves will do the same.

The life of a disciple consists of good beginnings, good intentions, some successes, some failures, and many detours along the way. Those on the discipleship road will need to be granted new beginnings and will need to take courageous steps as they return to the path of discipleship. For that we need each other.

Just as God went after the lost sheep, so we seek after each other. Sheep do not always wander so far away that serious measures need to be taken. But in Jesus' flock we watch out for each other as the shepherd watches out for us. We want to make sure that we stay together. We are not border patrols keeping the wrong people out or prison guards keeping prisoners in. When wrong steps are taken, we neither scold nor punish. Rather, we care for each other. We watch out for each other, lovingly and respectfully. We are not out to rob each other of freedom. We honor each other, but we also help each other. We reject the sort of individualism that says everyone is free to do as they please; we know it would be far too dangerous to live that way.

Jesus' parable assumes that we will notice if a sheep has wandered away. It assumes that it is important for us to stay together, that we very much want the wandering sheep back again, and even that the sheep would certainly want to be back in the fold, if only it could find the way. The parable also assumes that we know how to celebrate forgiveness, reconciliation, and new beginnings. On all these aspects of community life we are a long way from the goal. Our ideals for the church, and particularly God's ideals for the church, far outstrip the reality. But Jesus, whom God sent to win us back to the fold, is our model. If God is ready to throw a party when just one lost sheep is found, we too can celebrate our small victories in these matters.

Like a Gentile and a Tax Collector

> If another member of the church sins against you, go and point out the fault when the two of you are alone. If the member listens to you, you have regained that one. But if you are not listened to, take one or two others along with you, so that every word may be confirmed by the evidence of two or three witnesses. If the member refuses to listen to them, tell it to the church; and if the offender refuses to listen even to the church, let such a one be to you as a Gentile and a tax collector. (18:15-17)

We cringe just reading these labels. Some translations even use *pagan* or *heathen* instead of *Gentile*. And we know what the people around Jesus thought of tax collectors. Who wants to be called a name like that? What Christian congregation has the right to throw around epithets at those who do not stay in the fold? When we read the contents of these three verses we cringe even more. Who is claiming the right to define *sin*? Who has the right to confront another person for his or her behavior? Haven't we learned anything from the legalism and hypocrisy of the past?

Whatever others have done with this passage, I do not read this text as a roadmap leading to the exclusion of a sinner from the Christian community. In fact, exactly the opposite is intended here. From beginning to end, the goal of the passage is to do everything possible to win back a brother or a sister. In the Bible sin means "failing to reach the goal." When our actions and our relationships somehow miss the target, we do everything we can to help each other head for the goal again.

"If another member of the church sins against you, go and point out the fault when the two of you are alone. If the member listens to you, you have regained that one" (v. 15). This verse indicates that our goal is to recognize a failure and clean it up, without the rest of the community needing to know anything about it. Confidentiality is preserved. The goal is always reconciliation; we never try to set up the "sinner" as a bad example. Restoration is taken care of privately if at all possible.

In the NRSV, used above, the words "against you" qualify the member's "sins." These words are missing from many Bible manuscripts. There is uncertainty regarding whether they truly belong to the text. If these words are original, the text might actually be talking about a conflict between two people—perhaps a situation in which both of them think the other person is at fault. Jesus would then be saying that when barriers come between two people in the community, we should not simply accept that as a fact of life. Each is responsible to go to the other and try to clear up the problem. An unreconciled relationship will hurt the individuals and the entire community.

Even if the two little words "against you" do not belong to the original text, there remains the possibility that we are dealing with only a misunderstanding. Perhaps I have a critical attitude toward another person, so we attempt to clear up the matter between us. Of course, it may be that one person truly has seriously sinned, against me or in some other way. Even then I give my best effort to help the person. The attitudes that Jesus encouraged earlier in this chapter must characterize my approach if there is to be a chance of true success in winning my brother or sister back.

"But if you are not listened to, take one or two others with you, so that every word may be confirmed by the evidence of two or three witnesses" (v. 16). These "witnesses" could play a variety of differ-

ent roles here. If a serious sin has clearly been committed, perhaps they are people who witnessed the offending behavior. Their role is then to strengthen my attempts to win the person back: "We know what you did, and we are concerned for you." If the situation is a conflict between two people, the witnesses are present to observe how I am handling the situation. Am I just trying to justify myself? Am I being fair with the other person? Am I really trying to be helpful? Loving? Forgiving? The witnesses might also be there to help convince the other person that we really do want him or her back again; we all do!

"If the member refuses to listen to them, tell it to the church, and if the offender refuses to listen even to the church, let such a one be to you as a Gentile and a tax collector" (v. 17). Only in extreme cases, when nothing else has been successful, does the community as a whole get involved. But what kind of "church" are we talking about here? Remember that Jesus is still talking to the twelve disciples. And Matthew is probably thinking of the average-sized church of his day, which would have been about thirty to forty people meeting regularly in a home. In mutually accountable groups of that size, the church as a whole can effectively act.

But what do we do in far larger churches, where many times that number of people gather and where a significant percentage of them do not know (and perhaps do not care about) the person we are trying to win back? It is clear that in such situations "the church" will not be very effective in taking this next step. Thus we need home fellowship groups, leadership teams, and perhaps other structures to help us act in ways that embody what Jesus had in mind here. Moreover, it would be a terrible mistake if we started literally practicing Matthew 18:17 before making significant progress in living out what Jesus has just taught in verses 1-16 about our attitudes toward each other in the Christian community.

The church puts serious effort into winning back the person

who has wandered away. When every effort fails, we finally have the right to kick them out of the church, right? No! Just the opposite. We never seek and are never given the right to dispense with a fallen member. Rather, we take one more step, the most radical step of all, in our ceaseless efforts to gain the person back again. We treat them like a "Gentile" and a "tax collector."

Perhaps only I will view the person that way (note that "to you" is singular in Greek) or perhaps the whole church will. Either I or we will now treat this person like a Gentile and a tax collector. And what does that mean? It means that if all our attempts so far have failed, we try it the other way around. We no longer view the person as a brother or sister who is going astray; rather, we view the person as someone who needs to be won to the fellowship.

We have never given up wanting the person back in our community. But the person's unwillingness to listen to the church has distanced him or her from us. Note carefully that the person is not distanced because of the sin that started the process. Rather, we now need to treat the person the way Jesus treated tax collectors. (Remember that the author of this text, Matthew, was a tax collector himself!) We certainly do not despise the person; that was an attitude toward tax collectors that Jesus criticized throughout his ministry. Instead, we imitate Jesus and invite the person into our fellowship. We pursue friendship with the person, exuding love and acceptance as Jesus did. We gladly share meals with the person. After all, we are doing everything possible to win this person into the community.

It was not the person's sin that caused the break with the church. It did not happen because somebody missed the target. Nor is the person on the outside because the attempted reconciliation failed. What's more, the church did not cut off the person from the community. Rather, the person removed himself or herself by not listening to the church—by withdrawing from the mutual accountability that defines us. Therefore, we now accept what the person has chosen to become: an outsider to the community. We hope that readiness to come back will be the result of their "time out." We have never given up working toward reconciliation.

Of course, in our own unique situations we will need to devise the best possible structures and procedures to help us apply to our context what Jesus is teaching in this passage. We are not bound to the literal wording of this text any more than we should literally cut off our hand. Rather, this text communicates to us what is important to Jesus and what kinds of actions foster his ideals among us. The steps that Jesus outlines here are designed to emphasize

- restored and reconciled relationships;
- serious effort to help each other along the discipleship road;
- willingness to receive and to offer correction;
- integrity and as much confidentiality as possible in our efforts to win someone back;
- unceasing concern and concerted efforts to overcome barriers and restore the wholeness of the community.

To Do That, We Need Help

We are not the kind of Christian fellowship that can carry out these principles successfully. Jesus knew that better than we do. So he promised that we would be given whatever we need in order to practice what he taught. We are invited to take courageous steps in the direction Jesus has shown us, and he promises both his presence and his help. The following verses contain astonishing promises that we may draw on as we attempt to follow Jesus' teaching.

"Truly I tell you, whatever you bind on earth will be bound in heaven, and whatever you loose on earth will be loosed in heaven" (v. 18). We might ask, "How in the world are we supposed to practice what Jesus has just taught when we can't even agree any-

more on what constitutes 'sin'"? Jesus answers, in essence, "I will help you to discern which ethical norms you should follow." Church is not merely the place where the Word is preached and the sacraments distributed. It is the place where we make ethical decisions together, where we think together and decide together what it means to follow Jesus in day-to-day life.

In Jesus' day, *bind* and *loose* were technical legal terms used in three different ways to refer to ethical matters. A fourth use of the term had to do with "binding" Satan and then "loosing" (setting free) Satan's victims. There are other texts in the Gospels that use the words with this fourth sense (see Matthew 16:19; Mark 3:27), but it does not seem to fit well into the present texts. The three "ethical meanings" of this phrase can help us to understand what Jesus is getting at here. In first-century Judaism, people would come to the rabbis and ask them to "bind" or "loose" in any of the following ways:

- *Oaths*: "I have sworn an oath—bind me or loose me." This means that the oath I have sworn now proves to be a problem. Keeping it would perhaps require me to break a law, but breaking it is itself against the law. Am I bound or loosed? Should I keep it or am I freed from it?
- *Ethical decisions*: "I would like to do this or that. But I am unsure if the law allows it. Bind me or loose me." This means help me decide if my proposed action is prohibited or allowed.
- *Forgiveness*: "I have done this or that—bind me or loose me." This means help me discern if I have sinned, and if so, what I need to do to be fully forgiven.

Jesus is passing this kind of responsibility and authority on to the church. Of course, we cannot bind and loose by simply pushing personal opinions on others or by taking a vote. Just as the Old Testament law was the standard for the rabbis, so the teaching of Jesus and the guidelines we gain from Scripture remain binding for us. But it is our responsibility as a Christian community to seek the guidance of Jesus and the Scriptures and to try to understand how they can be applied to the situations we face.

If as Christ's representatives on earth, we can, in Jesus' name and in ways consistent with his teaching, reach a consensus concerning what it means to follow Jesus in our time and place, then heaven will ratify our decisions. That is the promise of Jesus. We receive God's support for the divinely guided decisions that we make together. Jesus certainly does not promise that we will become infallible, but we will do our best with his help. If we remain willing to rethink our decisions in case we are given new insights, we can freely and confidently live by our present decisions. We can be confident that they represent God's will for us, as we are best able to discern for now, until God leads us to new insight.

"Again, truly I tell you, if two of you agree on earth about anything you ask, it will be done for you by my Father in heaven" (v. 19). If we are serious about becoming the kind of community described in this chapter, we can be sure that our prayer life must improve. It is, after all, completely impossible to truly practice the radical teaching of this chapter in our own strength. About what are the two people in this text agreeing? Naturally not a new car or a pay raise or whatever they might happen to desire at the moment. Jesus is talking about the matters of community life. We pray for humility, for integrity, for readiness to be reconciled, for a love that flows toward others (including tax collectors), for openness to the insights of others (we need that if we are to bind and loose), and so on. Here the whole is greater than the sum of the parts. We join together in prayer as we seek God's help so that we can develop the attitudes and practice the reconciliation strategies Jesus' gives us in this chapter. And God will hear our prayers.

"For where two or three are gathered in my name, I am there among them" (v. 20). This is probably the best definition of church the New Testament has to offer. The church is where two or more are gathered in Jesus' name. While it is true that we gather with other believers on a regular basis, this verse is not simply about our "getting together." It is rather about the miracle that happened when God *gathered* us, when God brought us together in the name of Jesus. God has bound us together through our common relationship with Jesus. In this new binding fellowship, Jesus is present in our midst.

These words "among them" (or better, "in their midst") remind us of exactly the same words that were used for the child whom Jesus placed "among them" (or "in their midst") in verse 2. The words in the original Greek text are exactly the same. Jesus will be present among us not as a ruler forcing us to do what is right, but as a child, unprotected and dependent on us to receive him. When we receive each other, we receive Jesus (see v. 5). Then the one who is both our model and our Lord will be present among us, and we will know it.

Immeasurable Forgiveness

I've referred to many different attitudes that are crucial in any Christian community. One of them has not yet been explicitly cited, though it has been the underlying assumption of this chapter: readiness to forgive. Peter could easily recognize this assumption in what Jesus had just taught. Suddenly he asks, "Lord, if another member of the church sins against me, how often should I forgive? As many as seven times?" (v. 21).

Peter saw forgiveness as a responsibility, and an odious one at that. The parable that Jesus tells in response to Peter's question ends with a challenge to forgive from the heart. Those who forgive from the bottom of their hearts offer it freely, gladly, and often. They do not count how many times they have already forgiven.

It is ironic, I think, that we cannot be sure exactly how many times Jesus said Peter should be willing to forgive. In some translations we read, "Not seven times but seventy-seven times." Others read, "Not seven times, but seventy times seven times." That leaves us with a problem. Are we expected by Jesus to forgive 490 times, or would seventy-seven times be sufficient? The original text can be read both ways. The joke is on us if we think it is important to settle this one! The whole point is that nobody's counting. Have I forgiven seventy-seven times already? 490 times? 7,437 times? 16,295 times? We don't know. We don't care. We're not counting, not if we have begun to recognize our own sinfulness, not if we have begun to learn what Jesus taught in this chapter, not if we have tasted of the immeasurably great forgiveness God has extended to us through pure grace. If we have tasted this, we offer new beginnings to others in the Christian fellowship, not counting how often we have done it before. And we receive new beginnings just as often from others in the community.

Those who have tasted the kind of Christian fellowship Jesus describes in Matthew 18 know it is worth every effort to pursue this ideal and become the kind of mutually responsible, forgiving, and reconciling community in which nobody is just there for the ride. In such a community we participate fully. We do not live for ourselves, we do not hide our weaknesses and our temptations, and we do not close our eyes when others are falling away. We bind and loose, we talk openly and honestly with each other and with God, and we celebrate when a lost sheep is returned to the fold. In such a community Jesus is in our midst.

Discussion Questions

1. How does the rampant individualism of our society and of the church hinder our attempts to become a mutually accountable fellowship?

2. Which of the attitudes and practical steps examined in this chapter can help us to become such a fellowship?

3. Where have we experienced the presence of Jesus "in our midst" as we have sought to be a binding and loosing community?

For Further Reading

Birch, Bruce C., and Larry L. Rasmussen. *The Bible and Ethics in the Christian Life*. Minneapolis: Augsburg, 1989.

Dever, Mark and Paul Alexander. *The Deliberate Church: Building Your Ministry on the Gospel*. Wheaton, IL: Crossway, 2005.

Jeschke, Marlin. *Discipling in the Church: Recovering a Ministry of the Gospel*. Scottdale, PA: Herald Press, 1988.

3

What Constitutes a Biblical Ethic?

We need ethical norms and guidelines for life. As Christians we believe that God has given us the guidelines we need. We seek them in Scripture, where God's will is revealed to us. In fact, to recognize God's will in Scripture and to find appropriate ways of applying it in our personal lives is a significant aspect of what it means to be followers of Jesus. But how does that process work?

Some maintain that ethical convictions are something that individuals need to figure out for themselves. Each person is responsible for his or her own life with God. It is no one else's business, certainly not the business of the whole church. The way I choose to live my life is a private matter. Ever heard anyone talk like that? Perhaps you've thought the same yourself!

I belong to the Mennonite Church, part of the Anabaptist stream of Christianity. We Mennonites certainly have a mixed heritage when it comes to making ethical decisions. From the very beginning Anabaptist churches understood themselves to be mutually accountable fellowships. For them it was clear: how we live is in fact everyone else's business. Through baptism we obligate ourselves to give and take counsel from our brothers and sisters. We aim to find biblical guidelines *together*, and we hold each other accountable to live by our findings and decisions. That is one side of our story.

On the other side is a legacy of strict legalism and harsh church discipline. Some of us have experienced it; others have only heard about it with horror. We've become allergic to anything that resembles it. "Never again!" we say with emphasis. So we fellowship together but carefully avoid commenting on what might be right or wrong for other people, regardless of how diverse our views and our lifestyles may be. And now someone thinks we should be discerning together which ethical guidelines we are going to live by? No thanks!

And yet many Mennonite congregations (and also many others) are making serious efforts to address the burning ethical issues that confront us in our churches and in our culture. I suspect that the most radical thing I can say on the whole topic of responsible ethical living is this: "It is my business what you do, and yours what I do." Our sexuality, the way we handle our possessions, the way we relate to people, including our spouses, the ethical guidelines we live by, the choices that test them (at work, in school, in our free time, when we fill out our tax forms)—we should be willing and able to challenge one another and give helpful guidance on all these matters.

Not only that. We need to learn to speak far more openly about such matters, talking to each other about areas in our lives where we are finding discipleship difficult. We have the right and the responsibility to get involved in one another's lives and ethical choices. We are a mutually accountable community. That, at any rate, is what Jesus intended us to be.

If we are convinced of this and ready to work courageously toward this ideal, we will truly be living a countercultural Christianity. We will be swimming upstream in a world of growing individualism. Our lives will be in significant contrast to the lives of those around us. The contrast will not always be in our choices themselves, for some of our ethical decisions will be similar to choices made by others. The biggest contrast will be living by the bold belief that our ethical lives are one another's business. Now, that's radical!

How can we formulate ethical guidelines that are in harmony with Scripture and avoid strict and loveless legalism? My goal here will be to establish some basic principles of a biblical ethic that can help us as we begin thinking about ethical issues. What constitutes a biblical ethic?

1. A biblical ethic has love as its primary measuring stick. Because we love God, we want to live in a way that pleases God. Because we love other people, we want to help them find God's good will for Christian living. Our highest goal is not to find some kind of objective standard that defines everything as either right or wrong and then hold this up as a measuring stick for people's lives. On the contrary, we want to find the most effective ways of expressing the love we have for God and for the people around us—because God loved us first.

Now, that does not mean that "for love's sake" we will overlook anything and everything other people do. If we leave people in the dark about what God calls us to be and to do, or about what is right and wrong, if we pay no attention to the difficulties our brothers and sisters may be having on the discipleship road, we are clearly failing to express genuine Christian love. We need each other's help to live the Christian life, and offering help to each other is the loving thing to do.

2. A biblical ethic emphasizes mercy more than holiness. The pious religious leaders around Jesus quoted Leviticus 19:2 as often as they could find an excuse to do so: "You shall be holy, for I the Lord your God am holy." And because they made it their specialty to pay scrupulous attention to every little detail of the law, they believed they deserved to be considered the truly "holy" ones.

Even though Leviticus 19:2 is an important scriptural exhortation, as far as we know Jesus never quoted it. Why? Did Jesus not consider a holy life something to strive for? Of course he did. I believe Jesus avoided the saying because he was surrounded by Pharisees who misunderstood it. For them holiness was an external standard by which one could measure whether people deserved God's grace. They had built huge walls separating themselves from the "unholy" ones whose fulfillment of the religious rules was suspect. But Jesus came precisely to tear down such walls. He related to all the "wrong" people, pouring out God's grace on them even though it was fully undeserved (as grace always is!). It is true that Jesus once said to his followers, "Be perfect, . . . as your heavenly Father is perfect" (Matthew 5:48), but coming from the mouth of Jesus in the context of the Sermon on the Mount, this means something quite different from the Pharisees' "be holy."

When we attend to the context in which Jesus' command comes, we see that he is urging us to be merciful: Be just as generous with your grace as God is. Love all people, even your enemies. That is what God does, pouring down rain and sunshine on evil and good alike! (see Matthew 5:43-48; Luke 6:35-36). *Holy* does not mean scrupulously legalistic; it means set apart. According to Jesus, the characteristic that should set us apart is our readiness to pour out grace beyond measure, as Jesus himself did.

So, what does that have to do with a biblical ethic? Our goal must always be to provide help for others along the discipleship road, not to stand in judgment over their lives and choices. The goal is not to define for ourselves a "holy minority" that proclaims the unrighteousness of other peoples' lives and builds huge walls between those who live by our rules and those who don't.

3. A biblical ethic has the indicative as a basis for the imperative. This is the kind of language theologians like to use, particularly when describing Paul's approach to Christian ethics. We find a typical example in the letter to the Ephesians. The first half of the letter emphasizes what God has *already* done for us. We have been seated "in the heavenly places in Christ" (2:6); we have been saved by God's grace, independent of any "works" (2:8). It is all God's gift. In the second half of the letter we read, "I . . . beg you to lead a life worthy of the calling to which you have been called" (4:1). First God acts out of pure grace, then we live our lives in ways that please God as a response to God's gift. God's grace has made our salvation a reality (indicative); that obligates us (imperative) to live in a way that pleases God. We do not try to earn God's favor by being good. God's favor is a gift. But having been made right with God, we owe God our lives. We are called to live a life that is pleasing to God.

4. A biblical ethic maintains the tension between the "already" and the "not yet." Jesus proclaimed the kingdom of God, speaking of it as a kingdom that is already breaking into the world but has not yet been fully established. We are to be idealists. We are to establish ethical guidelines that correspond to the kingdom of God, which is already breaking into history. This means that our ethical norms will sometimes seem quite impractical in the so-called "real" world (though for us the kingdom of God is also very real!). We will often be out of step with the world's norms and expectations, but we live as a sign of the already coming kingdom of God. Our lives announce that there is another world on its way; we are bearing witness to its reality already.

At the same time we are to be realists. God's kingdom has not yet been fully established. In a fallen world full of fallen people—ourselves included, of course—there will be many difficult situations in which the "right" thing to do is not always clear. We need a great deal of patience and readiness to listen to each other.

Those who know nothing but "clear rules"—who never recognize gray areas and are never prepared to admit that real-life situations simply do not always fit into our ideal guidelines—are simply not living in the "real" world. The Bible challenges us to be idealistic, but it recognizes also that idealism does not always work. One day Jesus was defending his and the disciples' actions to the rule-oriented Pharisees. Exasperated with their orientation to rules, he said, in essence, "Did you never read about the time that David clearly violated one of the Old Testament laws by eating bread he was not allowed to eat? Of course that was okay under the circumstances; he was hungry!" (see Mark 2:25-26).

5. A biblical ethic is concerned more with the center of God's will than with the boundary line. We sometimes speak of "sets" (especially in mathematics). There are bounded sets and unbounded sets. There are sets defined by their boundaries and sets defined by their centers. A centered set, for example, might be the set of all bright stars; the brightest one of all would be at the center of the set. There really are no exact boundaries to such a set. A bounded set, however, defines precisely which objects are inside and which are outside.

A boundary-oriented ethic is one that uses clear boundaries to define exactly what is right and what is wrong. It can then be used to define precisely who is living righteously and who is not. From this perspective, I am without guilt as long as I make sure I never step over any of the boundary lines. Everything is cut-and-dried.

But a biblical ethic is not like that. It is oriented toward the center. The standard is to be like Jesus. Jesus stands in the middle and we move toward him, our model. We orient our lives around his teaching and his example. Jesus is the one who gives us the motivation and the strength, as well as the opportunity, to get up and rejoin the discipleship journey when we fail. When we fix our eyes on Jesus, we are not incessantly looking for boundaries and always checking which side we are on. We are not constantly asking, "Is this behavior still acceptable, or would it count as sin already?" To be formally "correct" or "incorrect" in our behavior is not our preoccupation. Rather, our concern is to move toward Christ and the life he teaches us to live.

6. A biblical ethic takes seriously the diversity in Scripture. If we want to discern a biblical ethic, it will not do simply to take a concordance, find all the verses that refer to a specific ethical issue, pull these verses out of their biblical contexts, and somehow make them all fit together into a consistent "biblical view" of whatever topic we are studying. I've seen people use that method. Recalcitrant pieces of the puzzle are twisted and turned and bent to make them fit with the others; that's necessary because the pieces really don't fit together very well. But with enough effort the pieces are all assembled into "the biblical view"; amazingly, it is often exactly the view the person held before getting out the concordance.

We gain much more help from Scripture if we recognize and value the diversity in the texts than if we persist in trying desperately to eliminate it. Reading each text within its larger literary and historical context reveals that texts on the same topic often say different things because they are responses to different questions and approach the issues from different angles. Often the Bible offers us so much more than a one-answer-fits-all response to every situation. What it offers is insight into how God views the topic at hand and various examples of how that might look in the variegated situations of daily life. Sometimes instead of the biblical *answer* we discover the biblical *approach*. And that is something we very much need to learn.

7. A biblical ethic is an ethic of the heart. Our actions are guided by our "heart"—by our basic orientation and inner motivations. If our righteousness is really going to be greater than that of the scribes and Pharisees (as Jesus said it needed to be—see Matthew 5:20), then that will not be possible by aiming to be even more scrupulous than they were. We will not achieve such righteousness by carefully orchestrating our external appearances, by accurately tithing our mint, dill, and cumin (see Matthew 23:23), or by counting exactly how many steps we take on the Sabbath. Rather, we are made righteous when we let Jesus transform our hearts so that we might learn to live as he showed us. Then love of neighbor and qualities like justice, mercy, and faithfulness will characterize our lives.

8. A biblical ethic is practiced concretely. A biblical ethic is an ethic of the heart, but it does not remain in the heart. It is practiced in the real world. Of course, we cannot take all the explicit ethical statements in Scripture completely literally. Not even all the exhortations in the Sermon on the Mount are to be taken literally. If I were literally to tear out my right eye and throw it away, I suspect I could still "[look] at a woman with lust" with my remaining left eye (Matthew 5:28-29). Not everything is to be practiced literally, but everything is to be taken seriously. Jesus meant us to find ways of practicing his teaching concretely, in the real world.

9. A biblical ethic is an ethic in continuity with the Old Testament. It is often claimed that the Old Testament is basically about law. If we want to find any grace, we have to turn to the New Testament. Some would be quite willing to jettison the Old Testament and attend only to the New. But Jesus spoke a different language. He clearly rejected the legalism of the Pharisees, but he did not reject the Old Testament. In fact the law of the Old Testament is deepened, interpreted, and newly applied in the New. As the prophets promised, its laws are now written on our hearts. We learn from Jesus how to observe the law without it becoming a heavy burden, how to truly experience it as Torah, that is, as God's guidance for life.

We know that many of the ceremonial laws of the Old Testament have reached their goal in Christ (for example, animal sacrifices) or have been declared obsolete (especially for Gentiles) in the Christian church (for example, cleansing ceremonies, food laws). But we will find a great deal of ethical guidance in the Old Testament if we learn to read it in light of its fulfillment in Jesus. For example, when we read the prophets alongside the Gospels we learn a great deal about what pleases God, especially regarding the use and sharing of our resources, care for disadvantaged people, and the practice of biblical justice.

10. A biblical ethic is an ethic of the community, not merely of the individual. Am I willing to restrict my own freedoms for the sake of others? Often the question we should be asking is not, "What am I allowed to do?" but rather, "What actions would best serve my brothers and sisters in the community?" For the sake of one of my friends I gladly offered to abstain totally from alcohol for the five years that I was his pastor. He requested that I do so; he was a recovering alcoholic and was having difficulty helping his teenage children, who were experimenting with drinking. Because our concern is for what helps others, we need to be willing to forego things we personally believe are not wrong.

But can we also turn that around? Can we free others to do what we personally believe is wrong? I think there are times when we also need to do that. I can clearly state my convictions, even explain why I am persuaded they are correct. But sometimes I need to rest my case, allow other people's convictions to help shape the ethical guidelines of my church community, even give the church the green light to make a decision I personally think is the wrong one. That too has a place in the binding and loosing community.

11. A biblical ethic is an ethic of cross-bearing. The cross is an important symbol of what Jesus accomplished when he reconciled us to God through his death. But it is also an important symbol for the discipleship road we walk, following Jesus. The discipleship road cost Jesus his life; we should expect that at times the road will be costly for us as well. God has not promised that when we live according to biblical ethics, our decisions will always "work." Followers of Jesus are not promised that if they live right, they will be blessed with a long, happy, and healthy life. The enemies that we are learning to love will not always be transformed into friends. Still we choose to take up the cross and follow Jesus as he invited and challenged us to do.

He will lead us along the right path—a path that may lead through difficulties, but always to the goal.

12. A biblical ethic is most clearly expressed in the Sermon on the Mount. Recently I have become more and more convinced that the Sermon on the Mount (Matthew 5–7) offers us a great deal of help in seeking to understand the nature of a life that pleases God. It will not answer all our questions, but it is an important starting point for ethical reflection and decision making. This text describes the life that kingdom people live. It is a life often out of step with what is "normal" in the world, a radical alternative to what human institutions and our contemporary culture call us to and reward us for doing. No wonder Jesus described his followers as people following a narrow path.

To change the metaphor, Jesus calls us to swim upstream, against the current. It is so much easier to swim downstream, to be carried along by the waters that surround us. But when the surrounding waters turn into a torrential flood and when it is our house built on sand that is being carried along downstream, we realize it would have been better to listen to Jesus' teachings (see Matthew 7:27).

E. Stanley Jones says it this way: "The Sermon on the Mount is not in our creeds. . . . Suppose we had written it in our creeds and had repeated each time with conviction: 'I believe in the Sermon on the Mount and in its way of life, and I intend, God helping me, to embody it!' What would have happened? . . . The history of Christianity would have been different."[2]

Discussion Questions

1. "It is my business what you do, and yours what I do." "We need to learn to speak far more openly about such matters, talking to each other about areas in our lives where we are finding discipleship difficult." How do you respond to these claims? What scares you about them?

2. Which of the twelve aspects of a biblical ethic presented

in this chapter seem particularly important or helpful to your congregation now?

3. What do you think of the idea that the diversity of viewpoints in Scripture is a blessing rather than a problem to be solved?

For Further Reading

Jones, E. Stanley. *The Christ of the Mount*. Nashville: Abingdon Press, 1981.

Sider, Ronald J. *Genuine Christianity: Essentials for Living Your Faith*. Grand Rapids, MI: Zondervan, 1996.

Talbert, Charles H. *Reading the Sermon on the Mount: Character Formation and Decision Making in Matthew 5-7*. Columbia, SC: University of South Carolina Press, 2004.

Part 2
Examples

We turn our attention to some concrete ethical questions. It will not be my goal to defend my personal views as vigorously as I can. There are already enough books written with that goal in mind. My goal is rather to provide a resource to help Christian churches take up the responsibility of considering these topics from a biblical perspective and looking for appropriate community guidelines.

In churches where a wide variety of opinions and viewpoints on ethical questions are represented (and that is beginning to be the norm), we want to bear witness to what we believe but at the same time allow our own viewpoints to come under scrutiny. It is important for a church to learn to live responsibly even when we are unable to reach a clear consensus on what the Bible teaches, on what faithfulness to Jesus means, and on precisely how our corporate witness to the gospel should look.

I am often asked, "What exactly is our *standard*?" Is it God's will? Is it whatever the Bible teaches? Is it the leading of the Spirit? Or is it the church and its attempt to reach consensus about all this? Is it our surrounding society, which partly influences us but in which we want to be good witnesses? Actually, all of these factors play a role, and we must be careful not to play them against each other.

Our standard is always God's will; that is what we are attempting to discern. We do so by first observing carefully what the Bible says—and *that* we do with the help of the Holy Spirit and in the context of the Christian community. If we want to discern appropriate *applications* of what we discern to be God's will, we need first to examine which scriptural teaching is clearly presented as unchanging, that is, as right and wrong in all situations; second, we need to examine which teaching seems specific to the context or the situation at hand. If we can determine that, we can ask what it means concretely to do God's will in our time and in our culture.

When we play these various factors *against* each other, many things can go wrong. If we take seriously only the written Word, we can develop a fundamentalist biblicism. If we overemphasize the binding and loosing role of the Christian community, the Bible's contribution can easily be squeezed out. We will end up simply sharing opinions and trying to work out compromise positions that we can all live with. If cultural relevance plays too large a role, the danger increases that we are led by the spirit of the age or that we develop a merely situational ethic. If in our Bible study we speak only of the guidance of the Spirit, we may be substituting subjective impressions for serious Bible study.

In the examples to follow I want to examine some controversial issues. I want to test suggestions as to how we as Christian communities can work toward ethical guidelines—and how we can do so with the Bible in our hands, with our ears attentive to the Spirit's leading, and with our eyes focused on appropriate applications in our time and culture. The "hermeneutical community" is not taking a position *above* the Scriptures when, after careful discernment, it makes decisions about what its position on a specific topic will be. Our goal is twofold: to take our time and culture seriously and to remain true to Scripture in applying its teaching to our world. In seeking to meet this goal, we may sometimes make decisions that differ from decisions made in the communities for which the texts were first written. When that happens, we should not assume that we have given in to a shallow situational ethic. On the contrary, we will have done our best at discerning God's will and applying it to our lives.

The goal of these chapters is not so much to provide definitive answers to ethical questions. The goals are rather to examine guidelines and principles that can be used in further reflection and to model ways of examining issues and of confessing personal convictions. In none of these chapters do I declare one position right and every alternative wrong.

4

Love Your Enemies

This chapter examines an important textual unit within Jesus' famous Sermon on the Mount and, on the basis of it, addresses topics like nonviolence, love of enemies, and the ever-controversial issue of military participation.

> "You have heard that it was said, 'An eye for an eye and a tooth for a tooth.' But I say to you, Do not resist an evildoer. But if anyone strikes you on the right cheek, turn the other also; and if anyone wants to sue you and take your coat, give your cloak as well; and if anyone forces you to go one mile, go also the second mile. Give to everyone who begs from you, and do not refuse anyone who wants to borrow from you.
>
> "You have heard that it was said, 'You shall love your neighbor and hate your enemy.' But I say to you, Love your enemies and pray for those who persecute you. So that you may be children of your Father in heaven; for he makes his sun to rise on the evil and on the good, and sends rain on the righteous and on the unrighteous. For if you love those who love you, what reward do you have? Do not even the tax collectors do the same? And if you greet only your brothers and sisters, what more are you doing than others? Do not even the Gentiles do the same?
>
> "Be perfect, therefore, as your heavenly Father is perfect." (Matthew 5:38-48)

Introduction

"There is so much in the Bible that I just don't understand," said Mark Twain's friend to him one day. To which Twain replied, "It's not the parts of the Bible that I don't understand that give me the most trouble. It's the parts that I do."

The text of Matthew 5:38-48 is one of those that seems to speak clearly. There are not a lot of complicated sentences; there's no difficult theological vocabulary; there are no mysterious parables; there are no references to obscure people, places, or objects. It just tells us how to live:

- Don't retaliate.
- Be willing to suffer persecution and insult.
- Be willing to be cheated both in court and out of it.
- Willingly do more for others than they even demand.
- Lend generously to anyone, even if you know you won't get your stuff back.
- Love friends and enemies alike; pray for everyone.
- Greet family and strangers and your sworn enemies with a friendly greeting.
- Bottom line: Just be perfect. God is!

Now, what could be easier to understand than that? What could be more hopelessly impossible to actually do than that? But precisely because the text seems to describe such an impossible ideal, scholars have gotten to work on it and ask all sorts of difficult questions that have made it, in the end, not only difficult to do but also difficult to understand.

Some say it is such an unrealistic set of instructions that it could not possibly have been meant for normal living. It must have been Jesus' special instructions for the disciples when he sent them on their preaching mission in Galilee, so that they would know how to deal with situations of persecution. It's obviously not for normal people in normal circumstances.

Some say you can't run a society on principles like that. Obviously it is meant for a temporary situation, when a crisis is on the horizon and heroic actions are needed for a short time, as in the crisis of Jesus' ministry or in subsequent crises like when Gandhi tried to persuade Britain to change policies in India or when Martin Luther King Jr. raised awareness of civil rights issues. But these principles cannot possibly work in normal life.

Others say that these instructions are for an ideal world, the kind of world that will exist after Jesus sets up his thousand-year reign of peace on earth. Someday the world will be the kind of place in which these instructions can be taken seriously and practiced literally. After all, it's a lot easier to turn the second cheek if nobody is hitting the first one, to lend if nobody has any needs anymore, and to pray for those who persecute you when persecution is a thing of the past.

And still others say it has nothing to do with how we live in the world. It has to do with personal Christian relationships. In the world, we live by the rules that make sense in the world:

- We retaliate, though we usually do it through legal channels, using the court system to get what we deserve and to make sure our enemies get what they deserve. There must be justice, after all.
- We insult back when people insult us—or at least we make sure we stay clear of people who insult us.
- We take care of ourselves and of our families first. We don't lend out anything we can't be sure of getting back, and of course we take security deposits before lending anything to strangers.
- We love our friends and make sure we keep a good distance from our enemies.
- And that part about being perfect like God is? Well, God's perfection sometimes expresses itself in wrath and justice and punishment of the wicked—sometimes even in the death penalty.

In the church, perhaps, we are willing to suffer wrong, but not out there in the big bad world. It just would not make any sense.

Finally, some say we cannot fulfill the impossible ideals of the Sermon on the Mount. Who knows that better than God? And that is the point of it all. God puts up an impossible ideal, we fail, and then we run to God for mercy. After all, the Christian life is about forgiveness and grace, not about living rightly. Nobody lives rightly. The more impossible the ideal, the quicker we realize how utterly incapable we are of living the Christian life, and the sooner we find refuge in Jesus, who lived the Christian life for us and simply asks us to accept his perfection by faith.

Well, by the time the scholars are finished with a text like this, the clear crystal waters have been stirred and muddied and mixed with enough theory that we cannot see anything clearly anymore! And so we just tuck it away and call it one of those difficult texts we'd like to take seriously, but we just don't really know what it means.

Well, let me suggest that there are indeed some things we can know clearly about this text. I suggest the following four points.

1. This is not an ethic for the world. Jesus is not trying to set up a utopian society or trying to enforce heavenly standards through an earthly political or legal system. He intends to transform the world by establishing an alternative society that lives by different values. That is why he addresses this sermon not to the crowds but to his disciples. The crowds are there and they are listening in, but Jesus is talking to the disciples (see Matthew 5:1-2).

Only at the end of the sermon does Jesus acknowledge that the crowd is listening in. Indeed, he makes his final comments to his disciples with that crowd in mind, confronting the crowd with the decision they must now make. Will they build their house on the sand? Will they listen to Jesus' discipleship teaching and then leave without committing themselves to his way? Or will they build their house on the rock by saying yes to Jesus, by saying yes to what he has taught his disciples? Yes in word and also in deed, in the concrete act of joining those who have stepped out of the crowd and now stand among the committed.

Jesus makes it clear that to be his disciples involves much more than accepting Christ's perfection by faith. He insists that discipleship includes hearing his words and acting on them (see 7:24). That is precisely what "the crowds" will not do. That is what disciples do. The crowds were astounded by Jesus' teaching. They were amazed at his authority. But amazement was not enough. In the end, each person in the crowd is confronted with the decisive question: Will I be a doer, and not only a hearer? Will I step out of the crowd and join the circle of disciples?

The Sermon on the Mount is not an ethic for the world. It is about how *disciples of Jesus* are to live. It was not designed to be a proposal about how a worldly society should organize itself. Thus Jesus' sermon does not mean that the world should

- get rid of the justice system (Why not just pray for evildoers?)
- get rid of the police force (Who needs it if we'd rather be hit twice than stop the criminal?)
- get rid of small claims courts (What's wrong with being cheated?)
- get rid of the army (We'll just let the enemies overrun our nation. After all, we love them!)

The Sermon on the Mount does not prescribe an ethic for the world. Of course the world would benefit greatly by taking to heart Jesus' instructions in the Sermon on the Mount. But Jesus calls for choice. He does not impose his ethic on those who have not chosen him. And he did not come to abolish the kingdoms of this world—not yet, anyway. He came to gather a community that would join with him and with each other in living in this world according to the principles of the kingdom of God. They will be out of step with the world's way of doing things, but they will be a sign that God's perfect plan is completely different from anything that can be imposed by force or by law or by armies in a sinful world.

Jesus did not expect the world to act Christianly. He came to call Christians to act differently from the world.

2. This *is* an ethic for the Christian community. Jesus meant for his *disciples* to take the instructions in this text seriously and practice them in life. They are the ones who have committed themselves to hear Jesus' words and put them into practice, like the wise man building his house on the rock. These are his instructions. These are the things he intends us to put into practice.

The ethic is for the Christian community; it is not an ethic for individual Christians to practice in the realm of their own private personal piety. Every line in these instructions is about relationships between people. It makes no sense to say, "Yes, I am committed to live by the Sermon on the Mount—but only in my private life." In my private life no one ever hits my cheek or sues me for my shirt. In my private life no one ever forces me to help them or acts like an enemy. These things happen only in my relationships with other people.

Moreover, it is only in community that we find the support and encouragement we need to take courageous steps toward living the ideals of this passage. I can refuse retaliation if I know that I have a supportive Christian community surrounding me and supporting my decision. My Christian brothers and sisters might even be willing to step in and speak to the enemy or at least to comfort the victim. It is a lot harder to do all this alone.

3. The Christian community that lives like this does so also in relation to the world. I said this is an ethic for Christians, not for the world. But that does not mean we live this way in the church and then live as the world does when we are in the world. We are called to live like God in an ungodly world. We are called to live self-sacrificially in a world that wants to take advantage of us for it. And the persecution and insults that this text talks about—well, I hope I am right in assuming that most of that happens *outside*, not *inside*, the community of faith.

The Sermon on the Mount describes how Christians live in their relationships with each other, but also how they live in their relationships with people in the world. That is what God does: God sends rain on the evil and on the good; God sends the sun to shine on the righteous and the unrighteous. That is the whole point of the passage.

Jesus said, "If you love those who love you, what reward do you have? Do not even the tax collectors do the same? And if you greet only your brothers and sisters, what more are you doing than others? Do not even the Gentiles do the same?" (Matthew 5:46-47). We will surely be living out of step with the world if we live in the world according to the principles of the Sermon on the Mount, but that is precisely what Jesus is calling us to do. We are out of step with the world, because the world is out of step with God.

4. **It is not an ethic of voluntary victimization.** Already in the Old Testament God began to reveal a strategy for disrupting the spiral of violence. "An eye for an eye" was often misunderstood to mean "If you do something against me, I am commanded to pay you back for it." God's intention in giving this commandment was to stop the spiral of violence by putting an end to the destructive power of ever-increasing revenge. The principle of an eye for an eye limited the violence and thus prevented its escalation. Only one retaliatory action was permitted, and it was not to be more hurtful than the original wrongdoing.

Now Jesus shows us an even better way. He wants his disciples to work for more than merely an end to the *escalation* of violence. He wants them to work toward stopping violence altogether. And the first step is to eschew violence themselves. Though that will not put an end to all violence, it at least has the potential for decelerating its course. Jesus calls his disciples to do their part, even if the ultimate goal is not reached. He uses some provocative examples to illustrate what he has in mind.

To highlight what might be the driving concern of this text, I share some interesting suggestions that have been put forward by Walter Wink.[3]

Holding out the left cheek. We can assume that the aggressor would strike me with the right hand, since the left hand was usually reserved for "unclean things" in Jesus' world. Therefore a slap on my right cheek would mean the aggressor was using the back of the hand. It's important to recognize that a slap with the back of the hand was an insult, an attempt to belittle someone or to treat that person with contempt. Dogs would be hit like that, perhaps slaves as well. So if I respond by holding out my left cheek, I am "inviting" the aggressor to hit me with the palm of the hand, as one would when picking a fight. And if I do that, I am standing over against the aggressor as an equal, making it clear that I too should be treated as an equal. Of course, I am not preparing to hit back, but neither am I allowing myself to be put down or to be treated as worthless.

Giving the cloak. Here the issue is a legal dispute. Somebody is attempting (presumably unjustly) to sue me for my shirt. Someone is trying to take from me whatever he or she can have. But I will go a step further, offering that person even my coat—something that could not be demanded. If I do that, I will stand there naked! And that is the point of the text. In that culture, if I stand before my opponent (or even in public court) with no clothes at all, that would not be shameful for *me*; it would be shameful for *the other person*, the one who had taken everything I had. To avoid this shame, that person needs to stop me quickly: "No! Don't give me that!" And thus, again, I become more than a victim. My opponent has lost power over me and is actually begging for my cooperation.

Going the second mile. If a Roman soldier wanted help carrying his pack, he was legally allowed to impress a civilian into service. He could require anyone to carry that pack a mile, *but no more*. If I refuse to set down the pack at the end of the first mile, it will surely look as though the soldier has not released me from my (forced) service. After all, who would believe that I was carrying it voluntarily. At the end of the first mile the soldier has no choice but to beg me to put down the pack; otherwise he risks getting in trouble. Now he is depending on my cooperation. Again, I am no longer a helpless victim of his power and his whim.

What is the bottom line? Jesus is trying to show us that he is not turning us into helpless victims by forbidding the use of violence. Rather, he is challenging us to find creative ways of working actively, but nonviolently, to stop the spiral of aggression and victimization. Even "the world" has seen examples of the effective use of nonviolent action—Gandhi's actions in India, Martin Luther King's in the American South, candlelight vigils in Leipzig, to name a few. Yet followers of Jesus are to choose nonviolence not only *because* it works and not only *when* it works, but because it is the way of the kingdom. As followers of Jesus we stand up to the aggressor—and all the more so when we are doing it not on our own behalf but on behalf of those victimized by abuse and violence. Turning the other cheek does not mean turning a blind eye. It does not mean allowing abuse to go on unabated. It rather means confronting it, but confronting it with a power greater than violence, namely the power of truth and of love and of courageous and creative acts of nonviolent resistance.

Yet, we must remind ourselves, Jesus is addressing the disciple community, not simply each individual disciple. Sometimes people who are being victimized are able to stand up to their oppressors with creative nonviolent action. Often it will be the responsibility of the supportive community to stand with those who are being victimized in interpersonal relationships or through economic, legal, and political systems. As a community we are challenged to think creatively how we might respond to injustice in ways that challenge without coercing, that work for justice without using violence to do so.

Now I hope that this next point will not cause us all to breathe a sigh of relief and quickly forget about points 1 through 4.

5. Not everything in the Sermon on the Mount is to be taken literally. That is pretty obvious in some places:

- Does Jesus really mean that people who have trouble with lust should cut out their right eye? Of course he does: he really means it, but he does not mean it literally (as though we would not lust with our left eye!).
- Are Christians really supposed to chop off their right hand if they commit a sin with it? Yes, indeed—but not literally.

Jesus intended the entire sermon to be taken with utter seriousness but not always with absolute literalness. Cutting out the eye and chopping off the hand really mean being so committed to a pure life that we cut ourselves off from those things that bring temptations and put us in positions in which sin is the natural next step. We take it absolutely seriously but not always exactly literally.

There are times when in this world we do rely on a police force and a justice system and laws that protect us from wrongdoers. But as we have opportunity, we show by our lives, our attitudes, and our prayers where our real priorities lie. We care about those who mistreat us. We show them acts of love when we can. If we must rely on the world's anticrime tactics, we do so not primarily to protect ourselves but to help the world be a safer place, a place where loving the enemy can be practiced even more radically. But this raises a difficult and much debated question.

Love of Enemies and the Military

How should a Christian answer when called to serve in the military? Should Christians be in the military at all? When Jesus spoke of loving enemies, did he include "national enemies"?

I come from a tradition that takes nonparticipation in the military far more seriously than much of the Christian world does. In fact, my ancestors were persecuted for refusing to join the military. My great-grandfather was shot at point-blank range, in the presence of his wife and children, because he refused to take up arms for his country.

If your viewpoint on this is different from mine, I hope you don't hear me saying that I question the seriousness of your Christian faith or the carefulness of your reasoning. I am not saying that; I am just saying that I disagree with you.

There are four answers I would give to someone who asked me why I would not join the military, and in particular that part of the military that produces, uses, or supports the use of weapons.

1. I can better testify that my real allegiance is to God's kingdom if I refuse to pledge ultimate allegiance to one of the kingdoms of this world. I want to live for God's kingdom and if necessary to die for it. Would I be willing to live and die for something that is a lower priority than God's kingdom, perhaps for an earthly kingdom? I do not know. I know that some people are willing to do so. But to kill for an earthly kingdom, that is another matter altogether. God is building an international and interracial church. As Christians, we belong to a worldwide family; we are bound together with all our brothers and sisters by our one Father. For me it follows that my ultimately loyalty can never belong to one of the kingdoms of this world—not to my homeland, not to my nation, not to any other geographical or political entity. When one of these kingdoms demands my ultimately loyalty, my answer is no. My loyalty is to God and to God's worldwide family. No kingdom of this world dare become as important to me as my brothers and sisters, who live in every part of the world. If it does, my priorities are wrong.

2. I would not want to risk killing fellow Christians in the name of my country. Of course we would like to respond that the Christians are on our side; that's why we fight—to stop the evil of the other side. Ah, if only that were true! In every war that has ever been fought in modern history there have been Christians on both sides. And usually both sides have claimed that their side represented the justice of God.

Mennonite Central Committee put out a powerful poster that had this simple message: "A modest proposal for peace: Let the Christians of the world agree that they will not kill each other." If we took that proposal seriously, no Christian would ever join either side, lest perhaps a Christian might also join the other side!

3. I would also not want to risk killing someone who is not a Christian and thereby eliminate any possibility of that person coming to Jesus Christ. Is it nobler to kill someone who is not a Christian than one who is, especially if God loves all equally and Christ died for all? Though it may be that from an earthly perspective the other person truly is an enemy, we need to be clear that this justifies nothing in the sight of God. We were God's enemies when God invested everything to win us back into friendship. How desperately our world needs examples of people who are willing to live the life Christ modeled for us—to love our enemies, whether personal or national. If Christians won't be those models, who will? We do not ask how lovable the enemy is, or for that matter how dangerous. We ask God how to treat enemies. God tells us, and God shows us.

My fourth reason for refusing military participation is the one I personally find most persuasive of all:

4. The New Testament teaches that Jesus' own attitude to violence is the model he asks Christians to adopt. When he was being treated unjustly, mocked, and crucified, Jesus prayed for his enemies. We are to do the same. He could have appealed to God to send twelve legions of angels to defend him, but he chose to suffer rather than inflict injury on others. The New Testament says that when Jesus went the way of selfless suffering, he was "leaving you an example, so that you should follow in his steps. . . . When he was abused, he did not return abuse; when he suffered, he did not threaten; but he entrusted himself to the one who judges justly" (1 Peter 2:21, 23). The New Testament teaches us to follow Jesus' example.

But many Christians respond, "Of course I would be willing to sacrifice my life, but I am not willing to sacrifice my wife and my children, my neighbors, my country. If I fight the enemy, it is not to protect myself but to protect the innocent. I am acting as God's agent to defend the helpless in the face of an enemy attack."

Now, that sounds very self-sacrificial, but it does not correspond to what Jesus taught or practiced. He did indeed stand on the side of the helpless, the victims, the vulnerable. But he never resorted to violence to defend them. Indeed he went the way of the cross precisely because he chose the route of nonviolent resistance to corrupt power structures. Jesus refused to call down twelve legions of angels that would have been at his disposal to protect him. He did not allow his disciples to fight on his behalf. He was revealing the truth about God's way in the world: God does not use military might to protect the innocent sufferer, not now that the Prince of Peace has come!

In every century since Jesus' day, the innocent have suffered. Indeed, dedicated followers of Jesus have suffered at the hands of vicious enemies. How often has God sent those twelve legions of angels to protect them with military might? Never. God chose not to defend Jesus with military power, and God has chosen not to defend Jesus' followers with military power, and God has not commissioned earthly armies to do so on God's behalf. God's way is the way of loving the enemy and, if necessary, dying in the process. That is what Jesus did. Jesus' victory came in weakness, not in power. We are called to follow in his steps.

Jesus did not come to set up a worldly kingdom, but to testify to the reality of a different kingdom. He calls Christians to do the same. When we adopt the world's methods of defending worldly kingdoms, it becomes difficult for the world to get his message. So we choose to die if necessary at the hands of our enemies rather than for them to die at our hands.

A Concluding Story

In the sixteenth century, a group of radical reformers, a tiny minority in their day, aimed to follow Jesus faithfully even when it led to conflict with church and worldly authorities. Among those who suffered for their faith was a Christian leader named Michael Sattler. His story was portrayed in the film *The Radicals*, which deeply moved me. Sattler and those around him were prepared to suffer unbelievably for their convictions and for confessing Jesus Christ. These predecessors of Mennonites and others in the free church tradition were models of confessing Jesus in an intolerant world.

After watching this film in a church, a man confronted me with a question that got me thinking: "Would you be willing today to allow yourself to be killed because of your beliefs about baptism?" My first reaction was, "No, I would not. I know what I believe about baptism, but to make it a life-and-death issue, to die for it? I don't think so."

But his question and my answer troubled me. I asked myself, "For what exactly were the early Anabaptists willing to be martyred? Was it really for their convictions about baptism?" No, it wasn't quite that simple.

They died because they were convinced, like Jesus before them, that true faith can never be promoted nor defended with the sword. And because they refused to take up arms against their enemies, they were vulnerable to death at the hands of their enemies.

What if that man had formulated his question differently and asked, "What if you had to choose between two churches? In one church people were willing to die for their convictions. In the other, people were willing to kill for their convictions. Which church would you choose?" If that had been the question, I hope I would have decided along with Michael Sattler. Thank God this is a decision that most of us are not required to make today. Our time is less life-threatening for us. We simply have to decide whether we will help defend an earthly kingdom with deadly force or follow Christ, the Prince of Peace.

Discussion Questions

1. "It's not the parts of the Bible that I don't understand that give me the most trouble. It's the parts that I do." What is your response to this statement from Mark Twain?

2. How do you respond to the claim that the ethic of the Sermon on the Mount is for followers of Jesus, but not necessarily always for the world?

3. Walter Wink proposes that in Matthew 5:38-42 Jesus is challenging his followers to seek creative nonviolent responses to evil. Jesus is not encouraging us simply to be taken advantage of, but rather to stick up for our rights and our honor in ways that slow down the spiral of violence. How do you respond to this suggestion?

4. Where would you draw the line in terms of participation in the military? Would you be a full participant, or consider only certain roles? Or would you not participate in any way?

For Further Reading

Roth, John D. *Choosing Against War: A Christian View*. Intercourse, PA: Good Books, 2002.

Sider, Ronald J. *Christ and Violence*. Herald Press, 1979.

Swartley, Willard. *Covenant of Peace: The Missing Peace in New Testament Theology and Ethics*. Eerdmans, 2006.

Wink, Walter. *Engaging the Powers: Discernment and Resistance in a World of Domination*. Minneapolis: Fortress Press, 1992.

———. *Jesus and Nonviolence: A Third Way*. Philadelphia: Fortress, 2003.

5

Sexuality

Sexuality is one of God's gifts to humanity. God's instructions on the use of this gift will occupy us in this chapter. In contemporary society, more and more people assume that an active sexual life is a normal and acceptable component of a love relationship between unmarried people. But what does the Bible say about that? And how should the church respond to the diversity of views people hold?

Talking About Sex

I want to begin, not by talking about sex, but by talking about *talking about* sex. Why is it so hard for us to talk openly and helpfully about the topic of sexuality? I suggest that there are a variety of reasons:

- For some the topic is taboo, especially in Christian circles. (They may have less trouble making suggestive comments or telling jokes with sexual nuances.)
- Often sexuality is considered a completely private matter. Many would say that what they believe about sexuality and how they deal with their sexuality is nobody else's business. "You have no right to meddle in my affairs, and I won't meddle in yours."
- Sometimes sexuality is seen as "bad," and I don't mean only

by those who have been sexually abused. Even Bible inter-preters convey this attitude. The truth is, Christianity has for centuries led people to believe that sexuality is necessary and permitted for procreation, but apart from that it is far more of a danger than a gift from God.
- Sometimes sexual sins have been so demonized—and sex-ual "sinners" so humiliated and ostracized—people have adopted rigid and anxiety-ridden attitudes about sexuality. It has became a topic one neither talks about nor thinks about (as if that were possible!).

Where sex *is* talked about, it is often a misunderstood and cheapened version of it that is under discussion. Often it is treated as merely a bodily pleasure one seeks in whatever way one pleases, wherever one can. Seldom is the role of sexual intimacy as a deep expression of love and faithfulness discussed.

It is not often that people feel the freedom to talk openly and helpfully about sexuality or that they discuss openly the biblical perspective on sexuality. Rather, we harbor our anxieties, our pain, our guilt, all carefully kept secret, and we keep our opinions to ourselves.

As a result, many people simply do not know what to believe about many aspects of the topic. My hope is that this chapter can help Christians talk a bit more openly about this topic and help them discuss appropriate viewpoints, recommendations, and guidelines. Of course, certain aspects of this topic are private con-cerns, for God designed sexuality to be something intimate. But to leave people completely on their own, expecting them to some-how come up with appropriate views and guidelines, can hardly be the best approach. We want to learn to talk about this.

Factors Shaping Common Attitudes Toward Sex

Lack of restraint. I am convinced that one of the reasons some people defend personal freedom to do whatever they choose in the area of sexuality is what I call "lack of restraint." It is part of a much larger human tendency and temptation to take advantage of God's good gifts. Our consumer mentality trains us to expect immediate and often disposable gratification, regardless of the consequences. We are tempted to grab for ourselves whatever enjoyment we can find in God's gifts without paying careful attention to the instructions God provided with the gift. If we unpack the gift and immediately throw away the instructions, we can do a great deal of damage to ourselves and others. We reject strict controls in favor of unrestrained freedom. But in the end we fail to enjoy the gift as God intended us to. It should be unthinkable for Christians to simply pursue sexual experiences with no thought of what God intended for sexuality. Sexuality is far too great a power for good and for evil simply to be set free to do its own thing, without paying attention to God's guidelines.

By that I do not mean to imply that people with no Christian commitment, who therefore quite reasonably have no interest in seeking biblical guidelines, are necessarily thoughtless and irresponsible. What I am suggesting is that people who claim to believe that Scripture reveals God's good will for our lives are being irresponsible if they ignore Scripture's teaching on this important topic.

In fact, I would suggest that the church is also being irresponsible if it offers individuals no help on the subject—no guidelines, no listening ear, no solid biblical teaching. People who don't find help in the church will find it elsewhere: from friends ("Others are doing it, so why shouldn't I?"); from the media ("Now, that's something I would like to try!"); or from the law codes ("It's not illegal, so why not do it?"). These sources of guidelines are always unreliable, especially when one's hormones are playing a more influential role than careful thought processes.

A negative view of sex. The unrestrained freedom to do as one pleases can go terribly wrong. But so can a legalistic set of rules, regulations, and prohibitions. This is particularly true because anxiety and misunderstanding often lie behind the rules and our fears of breaking them. Throughout the centuries, the church has typically adopted a thoroughly unbiblical attitude toward sexuality. First of all, sexual sins were considered far more serious than all the others, heightening anxieties when it came to sexuality. In addition, a life of celibacy was considered an especially high Christian ideal and, as a counterpoint, sexuality and sexual relations were seen as a necessary evil. The church claimed that conception was the only legitimate function of sexual relations. This understanding of sexuality was then defended with "biblical" arguments.

But even a casual look at the Bible should make it clear that these views do not accurately represent what the Bible says. The Bible celebrates sexuality and sexual relations. One need only read the Song of Solomon to see that the Bible has a place for the enjoyment of sexual intimacy. When we read this wonderful celebration of erotic love, we should not be too quick to declare it an allegory of the relationship between God and Israel or between Christ and the church. Its first and clearest message is obviously about a loving sexual relationship between a man and a woman. Even to accept it as an allegory only makes sense if a sexual encounter is viewed as a positive, intimate, loving encounter, not as a necessary evil.

A misunderstanding of Paul. Another factor contributing to an unbiblical view of sexuality is the influence of "incipient Gnosticism" and a mistaken "Gnostic interpretation" of Paul.

Gnosticism, as a developed system, probably did not exist before the second century. But its philosophical and religious roots were growing much earlier, and the effects of these were already being felt in the culture and the Christian churches of the first century. Gnosticism was (and is) a way of thinking that considers matter to be a weight that drags down the soul or spirit. The physical body, therefore, is a barrier that prevents the real person from truly connecting with the spiritual world. People influenced by Gnosticism tend to believe that all bodily longings should be repressed, that the body should be treated harshly, and that asceticism is good for the soul. Only in this way can the soul make true contact with spiritual realities.

In the first century, many people believed that by treating the body harshly and by focusing all one's energies on spiritual realities, one might be granted insight into the mysterious wisdom that would lead to a life of pure spirit. The goal of life is to rid oneself of the body's influences, a goal never completely achieved until one sheds the body at death. Thereafter the soul would be free of everything physical and would be able to find its true destiny in the pure world of spirit. (According to this view, a resurrection body did not make sense at all. Why would one want to have a body again, when one had finally gotten rid of the physical body that one had to struggle with all through life?) Everything physical was considered temporary, dangerous, and out of touch with God's ultimate plan for true human life. My sense is that Gnosticism is still alive and well (or more likely unwell!) in many places and people.

In Paul's day, another form of such thinking argued from the same starting point to a virtually opposite conclusion. Since the real person was the soul, some argued that the body was not really of significance to the true person. The body may indulge itself in any way it likes; after all, it's just the body. The important thing is to keep the soul pure.

Views such as these were widely influential in the Roman Empire of the first century and had significant influence on the church fathers during the third and fourth centuries. Unfortunately, Paul is often thought to have been influenced by such views as well, though only by the first kind discussed above. Paul was, it is claimed, arguing for a repression of bodily desires and therefore had a negative view of sexuality and, along with that, of women.

Thus Paul has been misunderstood and said to represent a view that goes something like this: Women are a serious temptation for men and often stand in the way of men reaching their highest spiritual potential in celibacy. Since not all men who aim for celibacy will be able to control their lusts, they should avoid fornication by choosing a lesser evil, namely marriage. At least in that context men can satisfy their (unfortunately uncontrollable) urges in a way permitted by God's law. Thus sexual relations within marriage is the alternative for those who lack the higher gift of celibacy.

There is, however, a much more appropriate way of interpreting Paul. He was in fact fighting Gnostic ideas and was arguing against its views on the body and on sexuality. Paul was convinced that Gnostic views led people astray in their thinking about right and wrong. He actually argued against both kinds of Gnostics—those who promoted asceticism that repressed physical desires and those who claimed that giving in to lust had no effect on the soul.

First Corinthians 7 is at the center of this discussion. The first two verses of the chapter are crucial here, and how one interprets these two verses can have a domino effect on how one understands everything else in this chapter about marriage, singleness, and sexuality. A literal translation of these two verses would be something like this:

> ¹But concerning the things about which you wrote. For a man not to touch a woman is good. ²But on account of sexual inappropriateness, each man should have his own woman and each woman should have her own man. (author's paraphrase)

Two crucial questions are, what does "have his own woman" mean, and whose opinion is being expressed in verse 1?

In answer to the first question, "have a woman" can mean either "marry a woman" or "have sexual relations with a woman."

Moreover, the word translated woman can also mean "wife." How we should translate the phrase "have a woman" depends very much on our answer to the second question above.

Consider the way these two verses are sometimes translated. Here is one possibility:

> ¹Now regarding the question you asked in your letter. Yes, it is good to live a celibate life. ²But because there is so much sexual immorality, each man should have his own wife, and each woman should have her own husband. (NLT, but other translations are similar)

According to this translation, the second part of verse 1 represents Paul's viewpoint. He is sharing his view with the Corinthians because they have asked or argued for something to which Paul needs to respond. Whatever the Corinthians believed, he believed that single celibacy is the highest ideal. He recognizes, however, that there is a significant danger of sexual immorality on the part of those who are not capable of living up to that ideal. So he recommends marriage for them as an acceptable but inferior alternative.

But there are more accurate ways of translating and interpreting these verses. Note the way the NRSV text is punctuated.

> ¹Now concerning the matters about which you wrote: "It is well for a man not to touch a woman." ²But because of cases of immorality, each man should have his own wife and each woman her own husband.

This way of reading the verses proposes that verse 1 contains not Paul's view, but rather the one that the Corinthians presented to him in the letter they wrote to him. Paul's own view is given in his lengthy response, starting in verse 2. The word *but* at the beginning of the verse signals a rebuttal of their view. Read this way, the Corinthians are arguing for abstinence from sexual relations and therefore from marriage. Paul is arguing *against* their view and saying that if people are pushed toward this option, immorality will be the likely result (or is already occurring). According to the NRSV, Paul is speaking *in favor* of marriage in response to the Corinthians, who are arguing *against* it.

There is, however, yet another way of reading these verses, and several commentators favor it (as I do). This third reading proposes that the Gnosticism of the Corinthians was leading them not only to argue for celibacy and singleness, but also for celibacy *within marriage.* They were arguing that a sexless, that is, platonic, marriage is the ideal for Christians, in order that the marriage might be "spiritual" and untainted by giving in to bodily appetites. They might even have been arguing that if a man has a hard time living up to that ideal, he can always find other ways of relieving his sexual tension—with a prostitute, for example. That way at least his marriage remains "pure" because a liaison with a prostitute would be better than spoiling his ideal marriage. Some Corinthians must have thought sexual relations with a prostitute were acceptable, for Paul had just been arguing against their view (see 1 Corinthians 6:15-16).

One might well translate 7:1 like this: "Now, in response to what you wrote in your letter, namely 'that it is good for a husband not to have sexual relations with his wife . . .'"

Paul's response? "That is no way to avoid immorality! On the contrary, husbands and wives should have sexual relations with each other."

Paul is in favor of sex, and he considers marriage a perfectly good and normal option, though it is "normal" only if one rejects the Corinthians' crazy ideas about marriage. Later in the chapter he will indicate that in certain circumstances singleness is a good, sometimes even preferred, option. But he will not do so because he wants believers to avoid sexual relations. That is not his viewpoint at all.

Paul's main point at the beginning of 1 Corinthians 7 is his absolute opposition to the idea of platonic marriage. He considers it a serious misunderstanding of both sexuality and marriage.

Sexual relations are not to be avoided; marriage should contain normal sexual relations. In fact, if we keep reading, we see that Paul reluctantly concedes that if the Corinthians want to refrain from sex for a specific period to give themselves to uninterrupted prayer, and if that is something that both partners want, then he is not opposed to this, as long as it doesn't last too long. Paul is *not* against sex. When was the last time the preacher in your congregation encouraged couples to have more sex?

In support of this reading of 1 Corinthians 7 is the fact that Paul addresses a similar situation in the same way in 1 Timothy 4:3-5. Here the ascetics were arguing for a strict diet and celibacy, while Paul argues for enjoying God's good gifts of food and marriage.

I propose then that we paraphrase the first part of 1 Corinthians 7 like this:

> You Corinthians claim that it would be a good thing if married partners would refrain from sex. That's nonsense. And you think that in this way you will somehow be avoiding something sinful or reaching a higher ideal. What a crazy idea! You don't even have to avoid sex while you spend concentrated time praying, but I guess if both of you really want to . . . just don't wait too long before you have sex again.

According to Paul, sexual relations are completely normal and good within a marriage relationship, but only in that context. It was the Corinthians who had problems with the topic of sex. Paul is arguing for a positive view. Sex is one of God's good gifts for married couples.

Sex Is Not the Highest Good

While neither Paul nor Jesus had a negative view of sex, neither did they teach that sexual relations are necessary to live a fulfilled life. Both made it very clear that the ability to be contentedly single, to live a fulfilled celibate life, is a gift from

God. That gift is not given to everyone, but those who have this gift are encouraged to give the gift back to God by devoting their freed-up energy to the things of the Lord (see Matthew 19:10-12; 1 Corinthians 7:32-35).

Sexuality is indeed a gift from God to humanity, but as Richard Hays writes, "the love of God is far more important than any human love. Sexual fulfillment finds its place, at best, as a subsidiary good within this larger picture."[4] Every human being is a sexual being; God planned it that way. Every person has a need for intimate interpersonal relationships; that too is a gift from God. But these relationships do not necessarily need to be expressed in sexual relations.

Sexuality, Unmarried Partnerships, and Church Membership

Our examination of basic biblical teaching about sexuality leads to a question on which the church seems to have lost its earlier consensus: in what contexts are intimate sexual relationships appropriate? More and more, people in western cultures have a ready answer: "Whatever context people want." Because that is a widely held view in our culture, and even more widely portrayed in the media, it is important for Christian churches to think carefully about the topic.

It is important to seek consensus. There was once consensus among Christians that sexual relations are forbidden except within a marriage relationship. There are undoubtedly still many churches in which one would find a widespread consensus that this is the only way the Bible can be interpreted. But there are a growing number of churches in which this consensus is no longer held and certainly not enforced. Perhaps only a minority of churches in North America have abandoned the traditional consensus, but certainly a majority of European churches have done so. In many churches there is not a realistic hope that the church will regain a consensus on the question, certainly not any time soon. In this situation it becomes all the more important to discuss the issue and arrive at some common convictions. If we cannot completely agree on what we believe, then at least we should talk about what we would recommend and what we can and cannot tolerate.

Congregations that lack common convictions on a topic lose their ability to deal with issues that might arise. And they lose their profile—people who might be interested in the church have no idea what we believe, because we ourselves don't. For a variety of reasons, we need to agree on some basic convictions:

- We leave people in the lurch if we have nothing at all that we can offer when church members, or our children, ask us about this topic when they are insecure or when they are seeking the Lord's will in this area.
- We lose the ability to deal with sexual sinfulness if we have never agreed on what we can and cannot tolerate in the church.
- We find ourselves in a difficult situation if people come to us wanting to be baptized or to join the church if they are practicing a sexual lifestyle that many in the church consider incompatible with Christian living.

It is *hard* to reach a consensus. In many places in the western world, sexual norms and forms of human partnerships are being reevaluated and redefined. Values are changing. The definition of marriage is no longer clear. What kinds of relationships constitute a marriage? What in fact is a marriage (other than a legal contract)? When does it really begin? More than one kind of partnership is now achieving legal status that at least approximates what people have traditionally associated with marriage. In Germany, people often speak of an *eheähnlicher Beziehung*, a marriage-like partnership. People are less and less convinced that legal marriage documents are particularly important. Many consider marriage an outdated bourgeois tradition.

I am not at all convinced that we should lay the blame for all this unclarity strictly on the culture outside the church. Countless Christians have had negative experiences with sexuality and/or with church people's attitudes toward it. Many have rejected the church and its morals as a result, though often without finding a better approach than what they have rejected. In many churches, members believe and practice a wide range of viewpoints, which has compounded our difficulty in talking openly and helpfully about the topic.

But isn't the Bible clear? Many Americans are astonished when they hear that some Germans genuinely question whether the Bible actually forbids sexual relations outside marriage. They often respond, "Well, of course it does; there are lots of texts that clearly forbid fornication." But when Germans look in their Bibles they do not find any of these clear texts. The reason is that English translations of the Bible typically "solve" a problem that German translations leave unsolved. The problem is in translating the Greek word *porneia*. Most times when this word is found in the New Testament, English Bibles simply translate it as *fornication*. Fornication is then understood to mean sexual intercourse between unmarried persons.

In German translations of the Bible, porneia is usually translated *Unzucht*, which means something like "things in the area of sexuality that are not appropriate"—without suggesting what those things might be. So in English, the "sin lists" of the New Testament (Mark 7:21-23; Romans 1:29-31; Galatians 5:19-21, etc.) include fornication, that is, sexual relations between unmarried people. In German the sin lists include Unzucht, that is, whatever sexual activities are sinful. So Bible readers who are not already convinced that sex between unmarried people is always sin will not automatically conclude that Unzucht refers to it.

So, what does the Greek word actually mean? Porneia sometimes refers to *any* sinful sexual activity (without specifying which ones are in fact sinful) and sometimes refers to a *particular* sinful sexual activity, such as incest. Nowhere is it certain that the word specifically means sex between unmarried people.

If the Bible clearly teaches that sexual relations between unmarried people are sinful, then fornication would be rightly included in the concept of porneia. But German Christians ask where the Bible clearly states that? One cannot simply assume the sinfulness of all nonmarital sex and therefore include it under porneia, and then in turn claim that the assumption must be true because the Bible forbids porneia. That is what Germans often claim (and not without some justification) is happening in the English translations.

This of course does not prove that sexual relations outside marriage are permitted. All it means is that we will have to look for some evidence besides the prohibitions of porneia. The presence of porneia on the sin lists does not make the case.

What makes things even more difficult is that some parts of the Bible seem to allow certain kinds of relationships and the sexuality that goes with them. These relationships fall outside the boundaries of what other parts of the Bible permit. In the Old Testament we find examples of polygamy (for example, Jacob marrying Rachel after marrying Leah); there are instances of men taking concubines, apparently condoned by the biblical author; and even prostitution does not seem clearly forbidden in some Old Testament contexts.

What this means is that if we want to find biblical answers to some of these questions, we will not likely be able to do so simply by finding a verse and quoting it. There are no verses that cannot be reasonably challenged or at least countered with what one finds in another text. What we need to be able to discern is the tenor of the Scriptures, the direction in which the Bible is pointing us. A biblical view will need to be discerned by taking seriously the Bible as a whole and finding in it a clear direction. We will need to discern what is clear in Scripture and use that as a guide in thinking through issues that are spelled out less clearly. When we have found what seems to be the teaching of Scripture, we are still faced with the question, what does that mean for us in our situation? That's a question we always need to ask, no matter what the issue. This is no small challenge, because many Christians are less than convinced that the Bible clearly forbids all sexual relations outside marriage.

So what does the Bible say? First, sexuality is a gift from God. God intentionally created humankind as male and female and brought the first human pair together to become "one flesh" (see Genesis 1:27-28; 2:24-25). The sexual nature of humans is a creative act of God. The intimate physical expression of human sexuality is to be viewed as a gift from God.

Second, God's design for sexual relations has at least three aspects:

- Through sexual relations children are conceived and humankind is thus enabled to carry out the first commandment of God: "Be fruitful and multiply, and fill the earth" (Genesis 1:28). It is the only commandment of God, someone has said, that humanity has successfully fulfilled.
- The most intimate of human relationships—marriage—is deepened and enriched through sexual relations. Thus Adam and Eve could enjoy their partnership in unrestrained freedom as they became "one flesh" and as they were naked together and not ashamed (see Genesis 2:18, 24-25).
- Through sexual relations God symbolizes the intimate relationship between God and humans. Marriage is often used in Scripture to depict the relationship between God and Israel. Adultery is regularly used to depict unfaithfulness to Israel's covenant relationship with God. The marriage bond, becoming one flesh, depicts the deep love between Christ and the church (see Ephesians 5:31-32). I would venture to propose that God did not merely find in marriage and sexuality a suitable illustration for the relationship between

God and God's people. I would propose that God designed marriage and sexuality so that humans might have something in their experience to help them understand God's love and covenant faithfulness.

So, what does that imply? I think it could be argued that all three of these aspects lend support to the view that God never intended sexual relations outside the marriage bond.

- God intended children to be conceived within a marriage, not within changing partnership relationships.
- Becoming one flesh, a common expression for sexual relations, is tied together in Scripture with leaving father and mother and being united to one's spouse—the biblical definition of marriage (see Genesis 2:24; Mark 10:8).
- The intimate covenant relationship between God and the people of God is regularly compared to a marriage relationship, not to some other kind of friendship (see Hosea 3:1; Ephesians 5:30-32).

Sexual relationships can have a very deep impact on those involved. Psychologists now recognize what the Bible also says: to engage in sexual activity can have a very profound effect on a person and on a partnership. The obvious implication is that to engage in sexual relations requires both responsibility and commitment. The very nature of a person and of a relationship is affected by sexual relations. That means neither that a marriage occurs when people sleep together nor that it necessarily should occur if they do. But it does mean that people often underestimate the profound impact sexual relations can have on a person and on a relationship. In fact, Paul goes so far as to say that a sexual liaison, even with a prostitute, is becoming one flesh (see 1 Corinthians 6:16). According to Scripture, sexual relations belong to the deepest level of interpersonal relations. In my view this should clearly bias us toward concluding that sexual relations belong within a marriage and only there.

As is the case with all of God's gifts, sexuality can also be misused:

- Sexual abuse occurs both within and outside marriage. Through sexually abusive relationships individuals can be significantly injured. In particular, the sexual abuse of children is extremely destructive.
- People can use sex manipulatively, within or outside marriage. When one partner demands sex of an unwilling partner, when one pressures another to do something with which the other is uncomfortable, when sex is withheld as a form of power, in all these ways and more, sexuality is being abused, with negative effects on the people involved.
- Irresponsibly conceiving children is a misuse of sex, often leading to rejecting the child before birth or neglecting him or her afterward.
- Casual sex in multiple relationships can seriously endanger a person's health, both physically and psychologically.
- Of course, sexual sins such as adultery, incest, and abuse are clearly forbidden by Scripture.

Sins in the area of sex can seriously damage people and relationships. Thus Christians should take very seriously our responsibility to search the Scriptures and the will of God in understanding our sexuality and what would be appropriate ways of expressing it.

But what about relationships that are clearly "like marriage" or "leading to marriage." If couples are engaged or if they are clearly intending their relationship to be a permanent one, what would be wrong with already engaging in sexual relations? That is what many people, including Christians (especially in Europe), are seriously asking. And the responses of Christians are no longer unanimous.

What happened to the earlier consensus? It disappeared! It was once considered completely obvious that according to the Bible all sexual relationships outside marriage were forbidden. Fornication, adultery, bestiality, or whatever other variations and perversions humans might invent are always forbidden, and when they occur are always sin. (I am deliberately leaving homosexuality out of this discussion; it is dealt with in a separate chapter.)

It is clear to all Christians (I hope) that adultery is always sin, but it is not clear to many Christians that sexual relationships in a partnership of two unmarried people is necessarily always sin. Most Christians would still maintain that sexual relations belong in marriage, even though society at large no longer says that with a very loud voice. But many who say that sex belongs to marriage are less than clear exactly what that means.

- Some debate when a marriage "really" begins in God's eyes. Some argue that this depends more on the attitudes and commitments of the people involved than whether a legal document has been signed. Many couples maintain that when they are engaged there is nothing wrong with sleeping together. The sex they experience already belongs to their soon-to-be-legalized marriage.
- Others are asking whether God could not recognize a partnership as a marriage even if the couple has no intention of going through the legal aspects.
- Still others want to open the question even more, especially if they are not convinced that the Bible, as we noted in the discussion of *porneia*, clearly forbids fornication. They would argue that in a partnership in which two people love each other, trust each other, are open to each other, and respect each other, a sexual relationship may also have an appropriate place. Some say, "Who knows? The relationship might turn into a lifelong relationship, perhaps even mar-

riage." Some say that even if it does not, the couple has not sinned.

What can the church offer? Because individual Christians hold a variety of viewpoints, so do the churches in which they participate. Few churches today ever test whether they still have a consensus, nor do they try to reach one. I think it is high time that churches initiate discussions on this important topic. But what if reaching a clear consensus seems unlikely? Do we then just give up and go back to silence? I think we can offer more than that.

The first thing we can offer is open conversation. Whether or not we have reached clear personal convictions and even if we don't all agree, we can talk honestly with each other, especially with people who are asking questions. We can give at least some sense of what is clear in Scripture and what may yet be discerned.

Learning how to share our convictions about sexual ethics may not be easy, but it is important. We may not all agree, but that is no reason to make sex a taboo topic. Our views may vary, but to dialogue about them is better than to fall silent. Silence will never equip us to address the issues that arise with our children, who need guidance, or with present or future church members who are living irresponsibly in the area of sexuality. Silence will leave individuals to figure out for themselves what guidelines they are to derive from Scripture.

I suppose there will always be sex in nonmarital relationships, but our silence about the topic will inevitably lead to one of two reactions. Some will *match* our silence: "We'd better make sure nobody ever finds out what we're doing." Others will *exploit* our silence: "The church has never agreed on any guidelines, so you have no right to stand in judgment over what we do." I can't imagine either of these approaches being healthy for individuals, couples, or churches. We owe it to church members and friends to provide basic Christian guidelines.

We had better be clear on one thing: people will be influenced by what they hear and see. If we as a Christian church will not attempt to have an influence on what our members or our children hear and see, influences such as friends and the media will be even more overwhelming. The truth is that we in the church have a responsibility to take seriously the whole counsel of God, and that includes those parts of Scripture that deal with sexuality.

Yet we must aim to offer more than a sharing of diverse views. Though we must respect people whose viewpoints differ from our own—on this topic as on every other—we also need to place a high value on the quality of our Christian fellowship and our witness before the world. That suggests that we should aim to reach a broad consensus in the church. What does the Bible teach about sex? What kinds of sexual activity are sinful? What church decisions and attitudes toward these issues will build up the body of Christ? What approaches to the discussion and what conclusions will enhance our testimony? Without placing a high value on these, our chance of reaching a consensus is diminished, and we will be unable to be helpfully involved in each other's lives.

Some Consensus Proposals

I am going to take the risk that I think churches should also be willing to take and propose guidelines for churches to consider. Before I suggest some proposals, let me put the discussion into context. My experience is that in North American contexts we all share a common tradition. A generation or more ago, there was a virtually unanimous consensus that no sexual relations are permitted outside the bounds of marriage. Many are not convinced that this consensus still holds. Many people support it neither in their convictions nor in their lives. The percentage of Christians who reject it is hard to estimate, in part because we keep our opinions on the topic very much to ourselves. Certainly more conservative churches would be closer to unanimity that the traditional consensus is a correct under-standing of the Bible and more liberal churches would be less likely to support this view.

I have also spent considerable time in church contexts in Germany, where far more Christians have abandoned the earlier consensus. Indeed, the earlier consensus would be hard to uphold in more than a minority of churches in Germany. In many churches it has been largely abandoned. I have heard church lead-ers say, "It is not our responsibility to teach our children that they should refrain from sex until marriage." In the churches I have most contact with, there is often lively debate on what the Bible really teaches and what diversity of practice should be expected or tolerated among church members.

My first proposal: Keep the consensus if it is still there. Any churches in which the earlier consensus can still be maintained and can be affirmed and supported by the vast majority of mem-bers would do well to teach it and expect members to follow it. The earlier consensus also corresponds to what I believe the Bible teaches. Of course, agreeing that this is the stance we will teach and expect does not automatically answer all the questions: What about the minority that does not see it that way? What about peo-ple who do not live up to the ideal? There might well still be sit-uations that raise tough questions. Nevertheless, churches that can hold the previous consensus would be well advised to main-tain it and use it as the basis from which to approach some of the tough questions. Churches that can keep the consensus will save themselves a great deal of tough negotiating as they try to work out what to do with their disagreements (see the proposals below). The challenge for churches that can hold to the consensus is to avoid becoming legalistic and judgmental in the "enforcement" of their consensus.

But what if the consensus no longer holds? Neither I nor any-one else has the right to assume that our own conviction is the only one that deserves to be heard and taken seriously in the church. The truth is that the earlier consensus simply doesn't reflect the beliefs of every Christian anymore. So, what do we do about that?

No doubt some will choose to attend a church that agrees with their viewpoint. But looking for a new church as soon as we discover a diversity of viewpoints in our present church is hardly ever a recommended approach. Finding a church that agrees with *every* conviction one holds is both difficult and dangerous—difficult because there are far too many issues on which people can disagree, dangerous because an enforced agreement on every ethical issue is a recipe for manipulation, hypocrisy, or legalism.

Some would like to go to the opposite extreme, choosing a church that never talks about any ethical issues, thus tacitly permitting everyone to believe and do as they please. But simply dropping the topic is also not a healthy or recommended course to take.

So keep the consensus if at all possible. If it is not possible, neither seek another church nor drop the topic. In fact, when consensus cannot be reached, it is even *more* important to talk together about the issues. In my view, carefully thought through guidelines and recommendations are all the more important when the actual convictions of individual members seem to be all over the map. What kinds of guidelines or recommendations might we consider?

My second proposal: Where consensus cannot be reached, work out guidelines and recommendations. I believe that as Christians we can begin by drawing a clear line between our convictions and a widely held view in our society, the view that sex is an acceptable activity in changing friendship relationships. According to Scripture, sex is more than "friends having fun together." I would hope that most churches could say that with conviction. Moreover, I certainly hope that all churches could reach a clear consensus that promiscuous sex, in which there isn't even a stable friendship at its basis, is a complete contradiction of God's purposes for sex and should clearly be considered sinful.

That does not mean that we should stand in judgment over our non-Christian friends who believe and live differently. Attempting to promote the Christian ideal in the world does not need to be a high priority for the church: "For what have I to do with judging those outside?" (1 Corinthians 5:12). People who do not intend to follow the teaching of Jesus or seek guidelines from Scripture will naturally find their orientation elsewhere and practice their freedom in ways Christians should not. We neither despise nor judge them for doing so, but we also do not join them in their decisions.

The question on which more and more churches cannot reach a clear consensus is whether *all* sexual relations that take place outside the bounds of a legal marriage are sinful. The teaching of Scripture is not unambiguous enough to convince all Christians that this is so. That, however, does not mean that the church cannot still be proactive in recommending a carefully considered sexual ethic and in establishing at least some boundaries on what the church will and will not tolerate in the lives of church members.

Churches that aim to draw some clear boundaries have several options they might consider. I would hope that all churches could agree that it is not acceptable for Christians to have sex in constantly changing friendship relationships. Many churches could go further by agreeing that not only in temporary friendships but even in more permanent relationships sex is to be avoided if it is not clear that the couple intends to stay together.

Of course many would like to go further than that, for they are clearly convinced, as I am, that an intention to stay together or even an engagement does not constitute license to begin a sexual relationship. Those of us who are thus convinced would wish that the church could agree on this as a standard. But we have to live with the reality that this is not always possible. In such a case I would hope that churches could at least *recommend* waiting until marriage. That way the church would at least be encouraging people to do what some believe is the only right thing and many others believe is an ideal to be pursued. The recommendation to wait until marriage could be presented as the "considered advice" of the church. In many churches, however, such a recommendation would have to be viewed as no more than good advice, for there would be many in the church who would oppose making it a rule or requirement. A recommendation is not a guideline that must be followed. It cannot be the basis for the practice of church discipline or for making a decision about whether or not someone can be baptized or can join the church.

My third proposal: In the absence of clear and strict guidelines, we need to be open and honest in our discernment of individual cases. If we will recommend, but not demand, that sex be reserved exclusively for marriage relationships, what will we do in the variety of situations that arise when members or people wanting to become members live out of step with the church's recommendations? I would suggest that those not following the recommendation be expected, at a minimum, to offer an explanation for their alternative choices. The church should take some or all of these steps:

- The church has a right to hear from these people why they believe that their choice to practice sex outside marriage is an acceptable choice. We may or may not agree with their defense, but if they have no defense at all, their attitude is exposed for what it is: "I don't care what God thinks about this, and I plan to do it anyway." That is in any case grounds for serious discussion about their understanding of the Christian life.
- The church should also be entitled to some kind of explanation about why the couple is choosing to live as though married, when in fact they are not married. So, in addition to answering the previous, they should be able to say why they

are choosing this course even though some in the church consider it a sinful choice.

- The church would also have the responsibility to make clear to those not following its recommendations that their example could very easily have a negative influence on others who might be far less responsible with their sexuality.

- It should also be clear to the couple that if they are claiming their relationship is "like a marriage," they should also consider themselves "divorced" if the relationship ends.

- The church also needs to be challenged to withhold judgment. If we cannot reach consensus and therefore have no "requirements" in this regard, we are not in a position to judge those who do not live up to our personal viewpoints or to our church's recommendations. On the contrary, we have the responsibility to be supportive and accepting of our fellow church members, even of those who live according to principles that we personally do not consider correct.

- My own additional proposal would be that a church seriously consider refusing baptism and membership to people who are living together and/or engaging in sexual relations if they cannot assure us that it is their intention to remain together.

- And the other side of the coin would of course be this: if we have only a recommendation but no requirement, those who are prepared to declare such an intention to remain together would not be refused baptism and membership if their faith and lifestyle are otherwise appropriate for membership.

- In every case, individuals, couples, indeed all of us, should welcome the caring, mutually responsible guidance we can offer each other on the journey of discipleship, even when we do not agree on the exact contours of the discipleship journey.

But what happens when an unmarried partnership ends, when those who lived as though married go their separate ways? How do we evaluate that and how do we respond?

- First, these relationship breakdowns should be acknowledged as failures. Just as those who divorce need to acknowledge failure, so also those who claimed a relationship "like a marriage" need to acknowledge failure when the relationship does not last.
- Second, the parting of ways does not in itself constitute proof that the couple was dishonest and that it was deceiving the church. Staying together might well have been their clear intention at the time.
- Third, the failure of their relationship does not mean that the church decided wrongly when it agreed to baptize them or accept them as members.
- Fourth, one should not necessarily assume that they wrongly decided not to marry. Sleeping together neither constitutes a marriage nor makes a marriage morally necessary.

What their separation means is more along these lines:

- It means that one of two decisions was a wrong one: either the decision to break off the relationship was wrong or the much earlier decision to live together was wrong. Since all our proposed decisions seem right at the time we are making them, such failed partnerships should add even stronger motivation to people to follow the guidelines of the church.
- No matter what went wrong, it is necessary to recognize and admit failure, to confess sins, to make restitution where possible, and to accept pastoral care in order to guard against making the same errors again.
- As earlier indicated, when "marriage-like" relationships fail, we are dealing with "divorced" people. (For suggestions as to what that means, see the next chapter.)

Some Final Personal Comments

I ask your indulgence if I make some closing comments that

reveal a few of my personal prejudices. I know that in doing so I risk being viewed as hopelessly old-fashioned or culturally insensible or terribly inflexible.

Often couples in love make the decision to sleep together "already," but "not yet" to marry. Other people might well ask, "Why are they sleeping together *already*?" (And perhaps at a later point they will ask themselves the same question.) I am tempted to ask a different question: Why are they not yet married? When couples that are in love and even already engaged wait years before marrying, or when they just cannot decide whether to marry at all, it is no wonder they are tempted to have sexual relations. When they do decide to marry, others often say, "You should still be waiting." Often I want to say, "You should have been married already."

Nobody needs to be able to afford new furniture before they are ready to marry. An expensive honeymoon is also no requirement for a valid or healthy marriage. What is my point? When I hear young people say they would love to get married and will as soon they can afford it, I am not convinced. Often I suspect that is a lazy excuse for wanting to have the privileges of a marriage while being unwilling to take on its responsibilities.

It is true that there are sometimes financial advantages when couples live together without marrying. A situation that I encountered often while living in Germany involved elderly people, usually a widow and a widower, who chose to live together unmarried. They knew that if they legally married, they would lose one of their social security checks. Marrying would mean choosing a lower income and a simpler lifestyle. But in most of the situations I have encountered, the issue is not financial need. The issue is living a simpler and less-affluent lifestyle. I believe that God holds out a blessing for those who do not over-value an extravagant lifestyle. And if some situations truly do involve financial need, a church might do well to offer the couple help so they can indeed marry.

I will take another risk that is perhaps the other side of the coin. If any readers have considered me too conservative in what I said above, here is their chance to consider me too liberal. There is one argument that is sometimes used to downplay the legal significance of marriage that I think deserves to be examined.

Some argue that the definition of marriage that is presupposed and built into our legal system has very little to do with the definition of marriage represented in Scripture. We should no longer allow the state, they say, to define for us what it means to be married. So far I agree wholeheartedly. A marriage comes into being through a legal act, but the law behind it does not define adequately what God expects that marriage to be. For example, there is no legal requirement that those who marry be sexually faithful to each other nor is there a legal expectation that the marriage partners intend to remain together for life. The law does no more than regulate the legal factors—such as property and inheritance rights, legal obligations, and family relationships—that come into play when two people sign the appropriate papers.

Some people have proposed a radical alternative to the current practice. If we really want to be a covenanting Christian community, they argue, perhaps the time has come to reclaim those Christian institutions like marriage whose secular counterparts have departed from the true biblical meaning. Why not dispense with "legal marriage" altogether? If a couple wants to acquire the legal rights that go along with signing marriage documents, that is their choice, but not the church's expectation. Rather, among its members the church should recognize as married all those—and only those—who have publicly committed themselves before God and the church to a faithful lifelong marriage partnership, whether or not they ever sign legal papers.

I can partly understand the reasoning. Moreover, if there really were a church in which such strong covenant relationships had developed that the church *could* realistically take on all the implications of regulating its own marriages (for example, regulating the rights of children, common property, and inheritance) then that church would have won my highest admiration. But I still think we should not move in that direction. I think the disadvantages would far outweigh the advantages. The time may come when we need to look at all the different legally defined relationships that are given the title marriage and decide which ones we can support as being acceptable Christian choices. But unless the situation becomes far more difficult than it is today, I think we need the larger societal laws to protect aspects of marriage that are not covered by good intentions and Christian support.

Who knows? Maybe the legal situation in some countries will someday produce a situation even more difficult to harmonize with a Christian understanding of marriage. I know that in some countries all sorts of different kinds of legal status are given to roommates, members of communes, various kinds of common-law partnerships, homosexual couples, and so-called marriages that are preceded with prenuptial conditions that cancel out the meaning of marriage. If things continue in this direction, the situation may truly arise when Christians have no choice but to opt completely out of the whole twisted system and decide for themselves which relationships they can consider to be marriage. I hope it never comes to that.

Nevertheless, we do well to consider carefully the significant differences between what the state defines as marriage and what God designed it to be. The first has to do with legal status while the second has to do with a covenant of love and faithfulness before God. In my view, the two aspects should not be separated. Together they form the context in which God intended sexual relationships to find their appropriate place.

A Word to Those Who Have Other Convictions

If churches take in members who live according to sexual norms that the majority of the church finds inappropriate, that does not mean that those churches endorse the alternative practices or declare them good and right. Rather, it means that we accept each other despite our disagreements on some ethical questions. Each person is responsible before God and the church to live according to God's standards as that person understands them. That still applies when we cannot reach consensus.

No case should automatically be viewed as a precedent that redefines the rules of what is acceptable. Rather, each member of the church and each person who wants to join it is an individual person whom we are obligated to guide along the path of discipleship. Their sincere desire to be a follower of Jesus should be clear to us so that we can wholeheartedly accept them into our Christian fellowship.

Discussion Questions

1. What traditional Christian teachings have been helpful to your understanding of sexuality? What are some of the ways the Christian tradition has been damaging?

2. How do you respond to the view that appropriate sexual relations belong only within the bounds of a legal marriage? Why?

3. Given the diversity of views and practices throughout the church, what are some guidelines on sexuality that would be acceptable to your church?

For Further Reading

Boteach, Shmuley. *Kosher Sex*. New York: Doubleday, 2000.

Foster, Richard J. *Money, Sex and Power: The Challenge of the Disciplined Life*. San Francisco: Harper & Row, 1985.

Hays, Richard. *The Moral Vision of the New Testament*. San Francisco: Harper, 1996.

6

Divorce and Remarriage

Divorce and remarriage are not merely abstract topics. They are real life issues for many people, including Christians. How does the Bible help us find answers for some of the difficult questions that surround these issues? How does Scripture provide help for people in difficult marriage relationships or for those whose marriages have failed?

So Many Questions

- Does the Bible provide any conditions under which married people may divorce? If so, what are these conditions?
- Is it even possible for divorce (a human action) to dissolve a marriage (a divine action)?
- From God's perspective, are divorced people actually still married?
- May divorced persons marry again? If so, under which conditions?

These are all *pastoral* questions. They affect many couples and are relevant to people whose marriages have ended or are in trouble. They want to know what options are open to them. These questions are also relevant for pastors and counselors who guide and support people through life's difficulties. For the Christian community too, as the binding and loosing fellowship that accompanies its members in the way of discipleship, these questions relate to its responsibilities of forgiveness, accountability, and support toward fellow believers.

The questions are also *ethical*. We not only ask, "What course of action is most supportive to the people involved," we also ask, "What is right and what is wrong?" As Christians we confess that marriage is more than a human or social invention, a contract between two individuals that we can define as we wish. Marriage was designed by God and is a covenant between two people but also with God, who unites the individuals in a marriage partnership. In asking these difficult questions, we are seeking God's will, not merely what we want or what the law allows.

The questions above are also *exegetical* and *hermeneutical*. Competent Bible interpreters are worlds apart in their understanding of the so-called divorce texts in Scripture. Every person and every couple seeking guidance for their own marriage situation can without much difficulty find a church, a book, a preacher, or a theologian agreeing with nearly any view they would like to believe. Not only that, but chapter and verse can be cited for the most widely diverging views in order to make them seem biblical.

Variety in Biblical Interpretation

"But the Bible clearly teaches . . ." How often have I heard or read that line? The sentence is then completed with the supposedly clear biblical teaching. And it turns out to be exactly the opposite of what the next interpreter claims the Bible "clearly teaches." Some texts clearly define marriage as "for life." They seem to forbid divorce categorically. Yet others seem to allow for exceptions and to regulate divorce. Precisely what the exceptions might be is an issue about which interpreters disagree widely. Moreover, they do not agree on whether possible exceptions apply to divorce only or to remarriage as well. Indeed, sometimes we cannot be sure whether a text is talking about divorce or separation or even breaking off an engagement. All of these could be called by the same name in the original language of the New Testament. Thus translations vary, and interpretations of the texts vary even more widely. It would perhaps be helpful at this point to provide a short and admittedly incomplete overview of the so-called clear biblical teaching.

Genesis 2:24. This biblical definition of marriage—leaving father and mother, cleaving to one's partner, becoming one flesh—clarifies various aspects of a marriage relationship. Jesus refers to this text when drawing attention to God's original plan for marriage (see Mark 10:6). Indeed, Jesus' interpretation goes further. He makes clear that when two people enter into marriage, not only do they and the society enter into a covenant relationship, but God is also active ("What God has joined . . ." Mark 10:9). But does this mean that a marriage *cannot* be dissolved or that it *should not* be dissolved? Does it mean that even a divorce does not end the covenant, or that humans *ought* not to end a covenant made with God? Here is where interpreters cannot agree, and the results have a significant impact on their beliefs about divorce and remarriage.

Deuteronomy 24:1-4. This text provides a set of instructions regulating what happens when a man divorces his wife (wives were not able to divorce their husbands). The man must give his wife a certificate of divorce. And he may not marry the same woman again if she has, after the divorce, been married to and divorced by another man. But much remains unclear:

- What is meant by the "something objectionable" referred to in verse 1?
- Why may the first marriage not be restored if another marriage intervenes? (Interpreters speak of the "kinship," the "dowry," the "legal-fiction" theories, and so on.)
- Can a text give us guidance even if we cannot determine

what principles were guiding the regulations in the text? Or is our uncertainty here irrelevant? Do we just say that biblical is biblical and do whatever the text says, even if we do not understand what it is trying to accomplish?

• Does Jesus declare this text irrelevant in his comments on it in Mark 10:5-6?

Matthew 5:31-32. This text seems to define an exception clause. The problem is that interpreters cannot agree on any of the following factors relevant to the interpretation of the text:

• Does it concern the end of an engagement or of a marriage? Both could have been called divorce in the first century.
• Did Jesus provide an *exception* or did he *exclude* one? The text can be translated both ways: "Divorce is not permitted, unless . . ." or "Divorce is not permitted, not even in the case of . . ."
• If there is an exception, does it provide a situation in which both divorce and remarriage might be allowed, or only divorce?
• Does the exception (if that is what it is) yield permission or merely limit the range of guilt? Put another way, does it say, "You may seek a divorce if . . ." or does it say, "If your partner destroys your marriage, that partner becomes guilty of adultery, but that does not necessarily make you guilty of it"?
• If there are truly exceptions to the general prohibition of divorce, how do we understand the texts that seem to deny all exceptions? Is it possible that Matthew is here reworking Jesus' words to fit his own context without being unfaithful to Jesus' intent?
• What is the meaning of the exception—*porneia* in Greek, often translated *adultery* in English?
    – Is the issue sexual unfaithfulness before or during an engagement? Breaking an engagement had serious

consequences in those days, and breaking the engagement could be labeled "divorce" (see Matthew 1:19).

– Does it refer to the "something objectionable" mentioned in Deuteronomy 24:1, which a man discovers in his wife?

– Does it refer to an act of adultery during the marriage? This is the usual interpretation, but is by no means the only plausible one.

– Does it refer to an incestuous marriage? That is, is this text about the dissolution of a marriage or an engagement that should not have been entered into because the partners were too closely related? At stake are the laws of affinity and consanguinity.

– And there are other options!

Mark 10:2-12. Here Jesus is answering a question by the Pharisees, who want to know which grounds for divorce he considers acceptable. According to Jesus, God's original plan for marriage (Genesis 2:24) takes precedence over the text they quote (Deuteronomy 24:1-4), a concession because of hardheartedness. Therefore, divorce and remarriage are not allowed. Among other issues, the following remain unclear:

• Does this text *assume, override,* or *explain* the so-called "exception clause" of Matthew 5? (How do we apply the principle that "Scripture interprets Scripture" in this case?)
• Is divorce excluded only if and when a remarriage is the intent of one of the divorcing persons?
• Does this text teach that concessions because of human hardheartedness are no longer valid?

Matthew 19:3-9. Jesus' comments here were again in answer to the Pharisees, and the answer seems to be a combination of his teaching in Mark 10 and Matthew 5. All the interpretive issues raised by those texts are also raised in this one. None of these critical issues are "solved" by this text (at least that would be the view of most interpreters).

Luke 16:18. Here the focus seems to be on a prohibition of remarriage. But it is unclear whether every remarriage is being excluded or only a remarriage in the situation alluded to by the text, that is, when a man divorces his wife to gain the legal right to marry another woman. Jesus' point would then be that a man is also unfaithful to his wife if he uses the legal route of divorce and remarriage to get the woman he really wants.

Paul's teaching. (See Romans 7:1-3; 1 Corinthians 7:8-16.) It is clear that Paul agrees with Jesus: God planned marriage to be for life. It is, however, unclear

- whether Paul's permission to "separate" under specific conditions means living apart or means divorcing;
- whether Paul believes that divorce actually ends a marriage in God's eyes;
- whether Paul was adding a second exception clause—that of one partner deserting the marriage—to the one Jesus gave—porneia, usually interpreted as adultery;
- and if so, whether we must conclude that there might well be other exception clauses;
- whether Paul's bottom line is actually something like this: there are no clear "rules"—each case must be evaluated on its own merits because "it is to peace that God has called you" (1 Corinthians 7:15).

Perhaps enough has been said to demonstrate that anyone who claims "the Bible clearly teaches . . ." is surely not correct. Unfortunately (or perhaps fortunately!) the Bible does not speak with one voice as clearly as some people wish it would.

What of the Bible's Diversity?

A large number of mutually contradicting books have been written claiming to have discovered the biblical view of divorce and remarriage. One need only examine a few of them to discover something interesting: they all use virtually the same method of interpreting the Scriptures, which I call the concordance method. One uses a concordance to find all the verses that contain the word *divorce*. Each becomes a puzzle piece to be laid out on the table beside all the others. The pieces themselves are examined without much concern for their original historical and literary contexts. Then the interpreter tries to make all the pieces fit together so that the correct biblical view emerges, and the problem is reduced to one of "difficult harmonization." So the interpreter sorts and arranges, bends and twists, until each text is interpreted in such a way that it does not disagree with any other text. Does the Bible allow divorce and under what conditions? Does that apply to remarrying? There must be *one* biblical answer, these people claim, and they are convinced they have found it.

There is enough interpretive ambiguity in the various divorce texts that it is indeed possible to make the most diverse viewpoints sound biblical by using the method I have just described. Here is a sample of the proffered biblical views.[5]

- *No divorce, no remarriage.* Neither divorce nor remarriage is allowed, no matter what the circumstances.
- *Divorce but no remarriage.* A divorce can be permitted under certain circumstances. However, the divorce does not end the marriage in God's eyes. Only death ever really ends a marriage. Remarrying after a divorce would constitute polygamy.
- *Divorce and remarriage in cases of adultery and desertion.* Remarriage is allowed only in situations where the divorce is justified by one of these two conditions.
- *Divorce and remarriage under various conditions.* A divorce is the burial of a marriage that has died. Various factors can

kill a marriage, and the persons affected are granted God's grace to begin again and to seek God's ideal for marriage with a new partner.

What Do I Believe?

Four experiences convinced me that there must be a better approach to this topic than simply to choose one of the four positions listed above.

First, I learned to know Lena.[6] She was trapped in a tragic marriage. She had followed well-intentioned but bad advice to marry "the better man" rather than the man she really loved. She had made some further bad choices in vain attempts to solve her marriage problems. She had given in to temptation and entered into a series of extramarital relationships. Lena in no way blamed her husband, Peter. Of course he was not perfect; no marriage partner ever is. But she knew that she, not her husband, was the problem. To the very end, Peter expressed his willingness to forgive his wife, to make a new start together, and to work on their marriage difficulties.

It was clear to Lena that she was living in sin with the extramarital relationship that her husband knew nothing about. It was a sin against Peter and a sin against God. At the time I was Lena's pastor. As we talked, she declared her willingness to take two weeks to consider her options carefully. She would read the Scriptures, seek God's help, and examine her own heart. Then she would decide what she was willing to do.

When we met two weeks later, she opened the conversation by saying, "I have decided to do as the Bible teaches. I've decided to live according to the teaching of Jesus. I will confess and forsake my sin and do what is right." In my heart I began to rejoice. But then she continued, "I have decided to divorce Peter and marry the man with whom I am having an affair."

I was astonished that she called this the biblical view and the teaching of Jesus. "And where did you find this taught in the Bible?" I asked.

"That is what Matthew 5:31-32 clearly teaches," she responded. "There Jesus says that divorce and remarriage are wrong, except in the case of adultery. My case is a case of adultery. So in my case divorce and remarriage are not wrong."

Her case was tragic, and her biblical hermeneutic atrocious. But this experience became an important "aha" moment for me. It was clear in an instant that she had read the wrong text.

You will no doubt respond, "The wrong text? Does the Bible have 'wrong texts'"? And I say, "Indeed! All over the place!" Every text can be the wrong text if we extract from it an answer to a question it was not intended to answer.

If only Lena had read Mark 10:2-12. There she would have found an answer to *her* question. There Jesus' questioners wanted to know what conditions would permit them to divorce the person they did *not* want to be married to and allow them to marry the person they *did* want to be married to. Jesus' answer is that there are no such conditions. That would be contrary to God's intention for marriage. Matthew 5 contains the text that Peter may someday need to examine to discern his own options, if indeed Lena decided to end their marriage through divorce. It does not contain an exception clause designed to justify Lena's intended divorce.

Is the goal to harmonize Matthew 5 and Mark 10 and interpret them so that they end up saying the same thing? Not at all. A harmonized version of the two texts might well obscure God's response to Lena's situation and to Peter's potential situation as well. The Bible does not provide us with a once-and-for-all, always-valid answer. The Bible gives us God's guidance for various situations.

Second, I took a close look at Mark 10:2-12. There I discovered that Jesus states perfectly clearly that there are right texts and there are wrong texts. Deuteronomy 24:1-4 was the wrong text for the question that the Pharisees were asking. Genesis 2:24 was the right one. The Pharisees were asking about the minimal conditions under which they would have the right to get rid of their marriage partners. What they needed to consider was God's intention for marriage in the first place.

Not all situations resemble the one reflected in this text. So Mark 10:2-12 does not provide the correct answer to everyone's question. Some people come to Jesus in desperation, fully convinced that God's intentions for their marriage are no longer reachable. The Bible has other texts that will help them discern the guidance of God for their life situations.

Third, I gave up the concordance method. Some Christians imagine that somewhere in heaven God has a special bookshelf. Alongside the Book of Life and other books mentioned in Scripture, there is no doubt God's original copy of the Bible, the one God dictated so that we could have a copy of it on earth as well. Among the other books would be one entitled *The True Theology Book*, another called *The True Ethics Book*, and so on. These books contain the "right answers" to all the questions we ask. We do not have copies of these books, but we do our best to reconstruct what must be in them.

According to this view, important but tiny excerpts from these books are embedded somewhere within the Bible. In fact, it is as if the pages of these heavenly books have been cut into tiny pieces and scattered throughout the sixty-six books of the Bible. Our job is to find the pieces that fit together and reconstruct the pages so that in the end our book contains something very close to what is written in God's heavenly books. If we match the pieces up the wrong way, we get the wrong answer. If we match them up correctly, we get the right answer, the one that is no doubt quite simple in God's book but for us scattered throughout the Bible.

According to this view, the goal never changes. We are always trying to find the biblical answer. With a complete concordance we can find all the pieces and with careful detective work we can figure out how they fit together.

This method is used over and over again, but perhaps most clearly and obviously when people are trying to find the biblical view of divorce and remarriage. Interpreters work with all the same pieces—the ones that the concordance finds. But they fit them together in such diverse ways that quite contradictory conclusions emerge, all of them dubbed the biblical view. Experience has demonstrated that this method does not work very well.

Try to imagine my children doing that with my words. Imagine them over a three-month period collecting all their father's sayings on the topic of candy. Now imagine them working diligently to harmonize all the sentences in which the word *candy* appears into one overarching theory. This they would then label "Dad's teaching about candy." The correct theory is the one that most successfully demonstrates a harmony of all the different sentences, regardless of the contexts in which those sentences were uttered.

The fact is, sometimes my children do something similar to that. One of boys comes to me and says, "Yesterday you allowed Benjamin to eat two candies after he practiced his piano. I just played piano. So now I get to eat two candies." (Actually he had pounded on the keys a little—he doesn't even take piano lessons! Besides it was ten minutes before dinnertime.)

Is it not amazing how easily we can detect the fallacy of such reasoning when our kids try it on us and yet turn around and defend it as a valid method of biblical interpretation? Does anyone seriously believe that this concordance method is a helpful way of learning *anything* important in the Bible?

Fourth, I was impressed with how strongly Jesus rejected rule-oriented thinking. What would Jesus do? This question is not always easy to answer, but it is always the right one to ask. If anyone thinks that Jesus' dominant approach was to promote one answer as always valid, no matter what the consequences might be for the people affected, they would be well advised to reread the Gospels. A good place to begin would be Mark 2:23-28.

The Diversity of Biblical Teaching Is a Blessing

It is precisely the diversity of the Bible's teaching on divorce that has become very important to me. Rather than offering a static moral rule that fails to address the complexities of life, this diversity allows the Bible to speak meaningfully to the diverse situations we encounter. Our task is to discern which texts address the questions we are asking in our particular situations. Every biblical text is a part of God's Word. Each text spoke a normative word to a specific situation. When we look for and take seriously the original goal of the individual texts, their literary and historical contexts, and the overall theological perspectives of the authors, we can hear God speaking through the texts into our situations. If we ignore all those factors, we hear God far less clearly.

The goal is not to find one always-valid answer. The goal is to learn to think biblically. The exegetical difficulties don't always disappear when we cease trying to harmonize all the texts into one theory. But we will be more honest and more successful in our search for viable interpretations if we stop trying to force each text to fit into the puzzle we have labeled as the biblical view.

So, What Is the Bottom Line?

Divorce and remarriage is a relevant and often painful topic, and the church often stands helpless after the fact, asking, "Is there anything we could have done?" We are often uncertain. What do we believe is right? How can we help people who are in marriages that seem to be falling apart? What are the guidelines we expect our church members to follow?

Below are ten points that I offer for consideration and discussion. These are not intended to be ten parts of the one right answer but factors to consider as we deal with various aspects of this topic in real-life situations. There is not room for detailed commentary on each point or exegesis of each text. However, after the seventh point I relate a true story that helps explain what I mean in the last few observations.

Point 1. God's original plan for marriage was and remains one man and one woman for life (see Genesis 2:24). That means we are all called to work toward the health and permanence of our own marriage and those of others. After all, God designed marriage so that it could serve as an image of the intimate faithful relationship between God and God's people (see Hosea 1–3; Ephesians 5:21-33). Our goal should always be to support, guard, and heal marriages. This involves offering and accepting marriage counseling, working at improving destructive behaviors, forsaking sin, seeking and offering forgiveness, and other efforts. (But see also points 7 and 8 below.) A great way to check whether we are really doing all we can is to take a careful look at the relevant chapter in Ronald Sider's book *Living Like Jesus.*

Point 2. The Old Testament allows divorce and remarriage (albeit polygamy too) in various situations. Jesus calls his followers to turn toward God's original plan for marriage, not to use Old Testament precedents or permissions as justification for aiming toward less than God's ideal (see Mark 10:2-12).

Point 3. We should not interpret the exception clauses of Matthew 5:31-32 and 19:9 as though they grant permission to divorce. Jesus is not teaching his followers that specific conditions give them the right to end their marriages. The exception clause was probably intended to limit guilt in situations in which one of the partners is unwilling to work at the continuance and restoration of a marriage. Marriage problems are never completely one-sided. This does not mean, however, that both partners are always equally guilty, that both become adulterers when a marriage ends in divorce. In the story of Lena and Peter above, the exception clause does not give Lena the right to end the marriage, as she claimed. But it also does not give Peter the right to end the marriage. Rather, it seems to be saying that Peter does not become an adulterer if Lena is unwilling to work at their marriage and decides to end it in a divorce.

Point 4. Marriages actually do end when a divorce takes place.

Here I am disagreeing with a view sometimes held, namely that divorced people are still married in God's eyes and that remarried people are therefore living in polygamy or permanent adultery. It is of course obvious that a marriage terminated by divorce is legally over. That is something that legislation can define for us. But it is my judgment that, according to the Bible, divorce also ends a marriage in God's eyes. Moreover, it does so even if the divorce should not have happened. Sometimes people violate biblical principles when they divorce and remarry, but they do not practice polygamy.

Point 5. After a divorce, there are a variety of reasons people should not remarry, at least not quickly:

- Divorcing with the goal in mind of marrying someone else is not an acceptable basis for seeking divorce (though see the story related to point 7).
- During a time of waiting, it might still be possible to reconsider and reconstitute a marriage that was terminated by divorce.
- In every divorce situation people need time to heal, to mature, to consider seriously whether they would be a better partner the second time around, and so on. Pastoral care and often therapy are important here.
- The Christian congregation needs to help discern whether a divorced person really is "marriageable." In normal situations, this would mean that the person has found healing and that the first marriage cannot be restored—that is, that the divorced partner has died or remarried, or that the "binding and loosing" community discerns that the first marriage cannot be restored.

Both Jesus and Paul spoke of singleness as a good and sometimes preferable option in order to serve God most effectively. Divorced people should seriously consider this option.

Point 6. In extreme situations, a divorce might be necessary to protect innocent victims, for example, of a violent husband or father. We want to affirm that marriage-for-life is God's will. At the same time we know that protecting people who are suffering from violence is also God's will. When these two principles come into conflict, we need to discern God's will in the particular situation. Honesty, integrity, discernment, and sometimes carefully developed hermeneutical skills are needed to find good solutions when biblical principles collide, when real people are caught in the middle, and when we see so clearly that a one-answer-fits-all approach is simply inadequate.

Point 7. People can get themselves into situations that are so entangled and confusing that it is no longer clear which relationship God would want upheld "until death do us part." Sometimes we need to ask in all seriousness, "Which 'marriage' needs to end, which needs to be legalized, and what is best for the children?" To clarify this point and prepare the reader for the last three points, I want to relate another true story.

John and Linda had started to visit our congregation. They were a lovely couple with two darling little girls, ages two and four. I wanted to win this family for our church, so I invited myself over to their home to get acquainted. We had a great conversation. Everything was relaxed and enjoyable, until I asked, "So how long have you been married?" I was simply curious and wanted to introduce a new topic into the conversation.

They looked at me, they looked at each other, and then John asked, "Do you want the short version or the long version?"

"I'll take the one you want to give me," I said, trying to make the best of a tough situation.

They told their story. John had rather spontaneously married a woman named Susan when they were both young, adventuresome, and reckless. Both were unbelievers and had no contact with any church. Six months later, their relationship was already on the rocks. They had no common goals and no interest in sticking it out together. Susan took off for England.

John found a new partner, Linda. They moved in together and soon Linda was pregnant. Two years later they were still together, a happy but unmarried couple, parenting their little girl and expecting another child.

That is when one of Linda's friends invited her to church. She went, enjoyed it, kept going, and soon came to faith in Jesus. Thrilled at her new beginning, she naturally invited John to come to church with her. He did, and through Linda's testimony and that of others, he also turned his life over to the Lord. The next step, obviously, was baptism and church membership, something both of them wanted. They wanted to live their lives in committed relationship with other followers of Jesus.

There was one problem: John was still married to Susan. So, what now? Of course John knew he had done many things wrong. Linda knew it as well. But what would be the right thing to do now?

Rarely, very rarely, when I have told this story, someone has answered, "It's clear what they must do. John needs to separate from Linda. He needs to try to find Susan and rebuild their marriage. Linda needs to have her child without John being there." Far more often, people respond, "It's clear that they have to bring the legal side of things in line with the reality. John needs to divorce Susan so that he can legally marry Linda, so that they can truly be the Christian family they have already become in God's eyes."

What would your congregation want them to do as they prepare for baptism and membership? Isn't it odd to tell someone that as a condition for baptism and church membership, "You first need to divorce your wife and marry someone else"?

What if John does indeed manage to find out where Susan is, calls her up to tell her what has happened, and explains that he needs to finalize their separation in a divorce. But before he can even begin the story, he hears Susan's astonished voice on the other end: "John! Is that really you? I can't believe it! I was just about to try to find out how to reach you. You would not believe what has happened to me. I've become a Christian, and God has given me a whole new life! I now see that I did everything wrong. I want to ask your forgiveness. I want to ask if you would be willing to try again to rebuild our marriage. I believe that with God's help we can make it!" What if?

Indeed, people can get themselves into such entangled, confusing situations that there is no longer clarity regarding which relationship constitutes the one they are responsible before God to uphold until death parts them.

And now the last three points.

Point 8. We need to avoid viewing pastoral solutions in difficult situations as precedents for others. Situations differ, and what is right in one situation may not be right in another. Yet we cannot do without guidelines. That's the tension we live in. We need guidelines and principles, and yet we need to be open to the possibility that the application of these principles will differ from situation to situation.

Back to the story of John and Linda. Where do we find chapter and verse clearly telling us what they should do? There are no such clear answers. What sort of church guideline might we want to construct out of this situation to help us in case we encounter a similar situation? How about this one: "If a man is married to one woman but has children with another, he should divorce the first and marry the second." (I hope none of my readers thinks this is a good suggestion.) No, John and Linda are a special case. Every other case is also unique. There are always similarities and differences between any two situations. One-answer-fits-all is an unsatisfactory basis for helpful ethics decisions on any topic.

Point 9. As Christian congregations, we are to accept and love people just as they are. We are to try to help them discover God's good plan for their lives and for their future. Whether we're married, single, divorced, remarried, or in a marriage that is on the rocks, we owe one another loving, merciful, guiding pastoral help, regardless of what might have happened in the past.

Point 10. Where the answers are not clear and people in difficult situations do not know which way to turn, the church has an important role. We are to be a mutually accountable, binding and loosing community as we make ethical decisions together.

The Bible can be a very great help if we seek in it God's guidance for life's difficult situations. In the Bible we find guidance about marriage, divorce, remarriage, pursuing peace, faithfulness and endurance, loving enemies, the grace of God, second chances, carrying each other's burdens, and binding and loosing. All these topics become relevant when people seek help for troubled marriages. The Bible helps quite a bit less if all we want is to find every verse containing the word *divorce* and then harmonize them all into "the biblical view."

Discussion Questions

1. To what extent should we allow our convictions on this topic to be shaped by concrete situations and specific people we know? Is it better to evaluate the biblical teaching "objectively"? Is that possible?

2. If you had been the pastor of the church where John and Linda became believers, what would you have advised them to do? Why?

3. Which of the ten points I have offered seem especially important to you? Which ones do we need to take much more seriously in order to become more and more "biblical" in our approach to divorce and remarriage issues?

For Further Reading

House, H. Wayne, ed. *Divorce and Remarriage: Four Christian Views*. Downers Grove, IL: InterVarsity Press, 1990.

Sider, Ronald. *Living Like Jesus: Eleven Essentials for Growing a Genuine Faith*. Grand Rapids, MI: Baker, 1999.

7

Homosexuality

Many people are insecure about the topic of homosexuality. In this chapter, I'll strive to avoid simplistic, unpersuasive, and one-sided arguments and provide a fair and honest assessment of what the Bible does and doesn't say about homosexuality. My goal is to help churches reach a healthy biblical assessment of current societal changes and develop appropriate Christian responses.

The Current Situation

In the western world, homosexuality is a much-discussed and controversial issue. Only two generations ago so-called homosexuals were despised, sometimes persecuted, and in some countries killed for their sexual orientation. Christian churches were in agreement that all homosexual activity is sin.

A great deal has changed. Almost everywhere consenting adults have the legal right to engage in homosexual practices. In some countries homosexual partnerships have been given the same legal status as heterosexual marriages. In some places in the United States, this option is being pursued despite a lack of clarity on the legal implications.

Churches are taking stands on these issues. Some are welcoming the legal and societal changes; most are vehemently opposing them. Some explicitly declare themselves "open and welcoming"; some produce hate literature and websites against these trends.

Some denominations are tearing at the seams because members disagree so vehemently on appropriate responses to these changes.

Even those who think they understand quite clearly what the Bible says and what God thinks of homosexuality are often unsure how to relate to people who maintain that their own very different stance is the appropriate Christian one. Many are asking how to gain consensus in the church or whether even to try.

The dominant trend in most western cultures is to promote unbounded tolerance and to celebrate diversity. The dominant mood is to declare each individual free to follow his or her passions without societal or moral restraint. But this trend is strongly opposed by those who argue that tradition, the wisdom of the past, or the "clear teaching of the Bible" should be retained, valued, and enforced.

Researchers who study homosexuality are far from unanimous on its causes, how those affected by it can best deal with its social and psychological effects, and which possibilities are open to them. In the churches with which I have had contact, I have detected much uncertainty regarding homosexuality. What is one to make of the vast diversity of viewpoints on homosexuality, and how is one to best relate to those affected by it when they are present in our churches or in our neighborhoods? The Bible is interpreted diversely, and many disagree about how to put into practice today what the various texts in the Bible teach.

The Language of Homosexuality

It is not easy to speak constructively about this topic, but not because it is taboo; in most places it has lost that status. Rather, it is difficult to discuss because one's choice of vocabulary is seen as already taking a stance. As soon as I begin to speak of heterosexuals as "we" and homosexuals as "they," it sounds as though I have already begun to do two things: (1) set up a "we" as the norm and "they" as those who violate it; (2) set up the dialogue as one that "we" will be carrying on about "them" because they are not part of the discussion. Neither of these ways of entering the discussion holds out much promise for healthy dialogue leading to insight and understanding.

My preference is for the term "homosexually affected people," which no doubt needs an explanation. If I were to speak rather of homosexuals, many readers or hearers would imagine I was already implying specific activities. Homosexuals would be people who engage in sexual activities with those of the same sex. Yet when I use the word *heterosexuals*, virtually nobody makes similar assumptions. Those heterosexuals who are not sexually active would no doubt be horrified if they thought that the mere use of that label stated an assumption that they were engaging in sexual activities with people of the opposite sex.

Some people prefer to speak of *homophiliacs*, from the Greek meaning "love for one's own gender," rather than *homosexuals*, meaning "sex with one's own gender." This would certainly be an improvement if it served to eliminate unwarranted assumptions about what people are "doing" and if it served to indicate that affected people truly can love each other deeply, whether or not they engage in sexual activities. The disadvantage of this vocabulary, however, is that it brings with it the assumption that heterosexuals do not or should not love people of their own sex or that they are not truly heterosexual if they do. The truth is that people can love those of both sexes deeply and that most people, especially men, should be encouraged to have more and deeper friendships with their own gender without fearing that they will be labeled homosexual. While it is clearly true that homosexuality does not revolve exclusively around sex, I am not persuaded that speaking of homophiliacs is an improvement.

If I chose to speak of people with a homosexual tendency or a homosexual orientation, many readers or hearers would assume I had already taken a stance on how homosexuality comes about. Is it genetic? Is it the unavoidable result of something over which the affected people have no control? These questions need to be honestly researched, not answered by default simply because we have chosen a vocabulary that implies an answer.

I choose, therefore, to speak of homosexually affected people to imply no more and no less than that these are people whose affections are such that they feel sexually attracted primarily to people of the same sex, regardless of what they believe about this and regardless of what they do or do not do because of it.

My Goal

Because I am persuaded that as Christians we have a responsibility to accompany each other on the road of discipleship, because I believe that what I do is your business and what you do is my business, because I believe churches should and can be ethically discerning fellowships, I offer the following reflections. They are designed not so much to see if I can persuade others to believe as I do but rather to help Christians and churches enter into constructive dialogue on this important topic. My concern is that churches begin to reflect on this issue before a concrete situation makes it difficult to speak openly and objectively. We shirk our Christian responsibility if our approach to or avoidance of this topic directly contributes to the secrecy, marginalization, and abhorrence of affected people, or, on the other side, to the silent acceptance of unbridled freedom for every individual to simply do as they please.

In my view the important questions that need to be carefully addressed include these:

- What does faithful obedience to God's will in relation to this topic mean?
- What helps individuals and what serves the welfare of the Christian community in relation to this issue?
- What enhances the testimony of the Christian church in the contemporary world?

As Christians, it will not do to speak only in terms of experience, scientific investigation, social change, or personal fulfillment. Our primary concern should be biblical exegesis, hermeneutical reflection, and Christian responsibility in this area. Discussion of human rights cannot be the final word. At the very least we must ask which rights and which responsibilities we are granted from a biblical perspective and not simply orient ourselves around societal norms and popular definitions of human rights.

There are enough books already designed to persuade the reader that the author's viewpoint is the only correct one. My goal in this chapter, as noted, is to facilitate fruitful discussion. I will not declare or defend my own personal convictions on every issue addressed along the way, nor will I attempt to adjudicate a "correct" response to various kinds of situations. I believe that at present it is more important that we as churches seek God's help in becoming a binding and loosing, ethically discerning fellowship. Whether it is realistic to hope that someday all Christians will come to a consensus I cannot say. But I am convinced that we dare not wait for consensus before opening up a dialogue and discerning how to approach the diversity of convictions among us. For these reasons I articulate a range of viewpoints that I ask readers to evaluate carefully without indicating why I consider one better than another or defending my own convictions. We need to learn how to enter into discerning dialogue more than we need to hear how one more author defends his or her viewpoints.

The Diverse Views

What causes a person to be or become homosexually affected? The range of views is astonishing:

- Homosexually affected people were simply born that way; it is a heavy burden, and they have no choice but to carry it.
- They are that way because God intended them to be born that way.

- They were genetically coded to be homosexual, and we should evaluate this neither negatively (first point above) nor positively (second point above).
- They have learned something that is sinful as a result of making ethically wrong choices.
- They are the helpless victims of emotional or sexual abuse other people have heaped on them.
- They have become homosexual because they have fallen under God's judgment.
- They somehow developed into the way they are almost certainly because of a combination of more than one of the above factors.

I strongly lean toward this last suggestion, though at this point I would not want to declare which of the other factors would most likely be the greatest contributing factors.

So, which options are available to homosexually affected people? Here, too, the viewpoints range broadly. To cover the spectrum one would need to include at least the following opinions:

- They should be free to practice that which corresponds to their affections.
- They should be free to engage in sexual practices within the context of a stable loving relationship.
- They should be free to engage in sexual practices only within the context of a lifelong commitment of faithfulness to one partner.
- They must refrain from all sexual activities and live in celibacy.
- Through prayer and therapy they should diligently seek to undergo a change of sexual orientation.
- They should live as though their orientation were heterosexual, possibly even marrying, trusting that their sexual affections will be reoriented.

- They should seek out a church in which their homosexual lifestyle is acceptable.

Naturally, one's viewpoint about the origins of homosexuality will influence one's sense of which options should be open or advocated for persons affected. Of course a number of combinations of the above suggestions could be considered. Still it is quite clear that the viewpoints held by individuals and churches cover a broad spectrum.

But what if we were to turn the question around? Instead of asking what options are open to homosexually affected persons, we ask what options are open to churches in responding to them. Here are some possibilities (not all of which I personally support):

- Keep a distance. ("We don't want any such influences around here.")
- Don't ask; don't tell. ("That is a private matter. After all, we don't speak openly about heterosexuality, do we?")
- Reject all homosexual behavior, but welcome the affected persons.
- Create space for open acceptance of homosexuals as we do for heterosexuals.

Clearly there is a range of views. Yet perhaps more troubling than this is the fact that people advocating their particular approach often claim to be presenting the view that represents what God wills and what the Bible teaches. It is clear that the topic needs to be addressed.

Three Proposals

As an introduction to a discussion, consider three proposals formulated by the Evangelical Lutheran Church in America.[7] The concrete question addressed here is, what does it mean to "love one's neighbor" when that person is affected homosexually?

Viewpoint 1. "To love our neighbor who is homosexual means to love the sinner but to hate the sin. The church should be loving and accepting of persons who are homosexual, welcoming them as members, but clearly oppose their being sexually active. All such activity is contrary to God's law. Negative moral judgments should be upheld and homosexual persons expected to abstain from sexual activity. Repentance should be expected from those who do not abstain, trusting that out of divine grace God will forgive them, as God does all repentant sinners."

Comments. In this view the tendency or temptation toward homosexual activities is viewed as either a perversion or sickness, in some way linked to the Fall. Many who endorse this view believe that homosexuality can be healed and that the affected persons can become heterosexual. To love one's neighbor here would mean encouraging and supporting people as they seek to overcome their homosexuality. Others would be inclined to accept the fact of one's homosexuality as a given and would then expect from affected people a celibate life.

Viewpoint 2. "To love our neighbor means to be compassionate toward gay and lesbian persons, understanding the dilemma facing those who do not have the gift of celibacy. It is unloving to insist upon lifelong abstinence for all persons whose homosexual orientation is an integrated aspect of who they are. To tell them they will never be able to live out who they are as sexual beings is cruel, not loving. Thus, the loving response is to tolerate, perhaps even support mutually loving, committed gay and lesbian relationships."

Comments. Most of those who take this standpoint consider homosexually affected people to be victims in a broken world. Though many would not go so far as to say that God intended what these people experience, they also say that in a fallen world one needs to be both compassionate and realistic. We must accept what cannot be changed. Viewing complete abstinence from sexual activity as an ideal that not all can achieve, many would encourage affected people to live in faithful partnerships. That, at any rate, is a better way to live out one's destiny than in secret loneliness or in constantly changing relationships. Some would see this option as morally equivalent to something like divorce and remarriage—that is, not what God originally intended but in some situations unavoidable or necessary.

Viewpoint 3. "To love our neighbor means open affirmation of gay and lesbian persons and their mutually loving, just, committed relationships of fidelity. Such relationships are the context for sexual activity that can be expressive of love for one another. Prohibiting this expression of love is incompatible with the love of God we know through Jesus Christ, who challenged religious rules that hindered love for the neighbor. God's redemptive and sanctifying activity empowers gay and lesbian Christians to live lives of responsible freedom, including through faithful, committed sexual relationships. It is untenable to maintain that those who are gay or lesbian should have to live lives of secrecy, deception, or loneliness, alienated from self, others, and God."

Comments. Those who hold to this viewpoint usually consider homosexuality as a valid alternative to heterosexuality. For those affected it is just as natural and just as God-intended as heterosexuality is for the others. Homosexually oriented people are no more and no less responsible for their sexual choices than heterosexually oriented people. Churches should be as ready and open to bless homosexual as heterosexual partnerships. Those holding to this view reject the idea that the majority determines what is normal (as in corresponding to a valid norm). After all, left-handers are also a relatively small minority, but being left-handed is no more contrary to nature than being right-handed. For what it is worth, homosexuality also occurs in the animal world.

What These Views Have in Common

Some would say these views are simply worlds apart with nothing in common. Yet they do have some commonalities. All three exclude the idea that people should be free to do whatever they want. Promiscuity is not an option in any of the viewpoints. All agree that there are appropriate and inappropriate behaviors, that people are responsible to seek and do what is right, and that it matters what we do and what others do. All three viewpoints assume that we are responsible for practicing appropriate behavior regardless of what factors have made us who we are. The fact that people may not freely choose their sexual affections does not release them from an obligation to do what is right.

Moreover, all three viewpoints require that Christian communities act responsibly in the way we respond to and accompany affected persons. All three views clearly state or imply that rejecting homosexually affected people or excluding them from our circle is not appropriate. We are called to love them as we love ourselves and to find appropriate ways of making that concrete. So whether people view homosexuality as a disease, a destiny, or a design, their obligation is to view those affected as people loved by God to whom we owe Christian love.

I think that if we were to talk openly and honestly with each other, we would discover that in most churches are representatives of all the viewpoints we have discussed. My own conviction is that, given the diversity of views Christian people hold on these matters, if we are going to err, we should err on the side of mercy, especially in those situations where homosexually affected people have already been despised by others.

What the Bible Says

According to many people, the Bible clearly teaches what we should believe about homosexuality. Unfortunately, what seems so clear to some people is far from clear to others. To examine what is there, I'll begin with this overview of what people claim the Bible teaches or implies.

First, there are only negative references to homosexual activity in Scripture. Nowhere in Scripture is the subject viewed as either neutral or positive. Nowhere is there a celebration of it. Some interpreters see one possible exception in the relationship between David and Jonathan. Based on the descriptions of their relationship in 1 Samuel 18:1-4; 19:1; 20:17, 41; and 2 Samuel 1:26, some claim that these two men had a homosexual relationship and that the Bible presents it in a positive and affirming light. The problem is that when we examine all other references to these two men, we find no evidence whatsoever that either of them was homosexually affected, and we find considerable evidence that they were not. Though the texts cited above may contain unusual descriptions of a relationship between two men, that is a culturally conditioned interpretation. Our culture may be more restrained in how men show affection to each other than other cultures, particularly the one in which the texts were written. I personally find little basis for considering these texts to be either a description or an affirmation of a homosexual relationship.

But if we remove these texts from the discussion, we come back to the main point that homosexual relationships, though referred to at various places in Scripture, are never described in a positive light. Either they are explicitly forbidden (see Leviticus 18:22; 20:13) or they are listed along with other types of sin (see 1 Corinthians 6:9-11; 1 Timothy 1:10) or they are presented as departing from the norms of God's creation (see Romans 1:26-27). Genesis 19:1-13 seems to refer to homosexual gang rape, though it does not actually take place.

Second, there is no text in all of Scripture that speaks of a homosexual orientation. Not until the nineteenth century was there any discussion or analysis of a homosexual orientation, that is, a sexual attraction experienced regularly by someone toward others of the same sex. It is now recognized, as it was not before the nineteenth century, that whatever the causes may be, those affected experience their orientation as a part of who they are and not as something they have chosen. At any rate, we have no literature from ancient times reflecting any awareness of homosexual orientation. Neither in Hebrew nor Greek, the languages of the Old and New Testaments, is there a word that corresponds to our idea of homosexual orientation. Nor is the notion of a homosexual partnership ever discussed in Scripture. It seems that in ancient times people simply assumed that essentially heterosexual people practiced homosexual activities because they wanted to broaden their range of sexual experiences, as they might also choose to do in various other ways that people would consider unnatural.

Many interpreters draw exactly opposite conclusions from these first two points. Some reason that it is natural that the Bible speaks only negatively about homosexuality. That is because there is nothing positive to say about it. And the Bible shows no interest in the topic of a homosexual orientation or tendency because these are completely irrelevant to the issue. Homosexual relationships are always sinful, no matter what factors might contribute to someone's desire for them. The biblical texts are clear that homosexuality is sin. Alternative interpretations of the relevant texts are misguided attempts to sidestep the plain meaning of Scripture.

Others reason that the Bible is silent on the question we seek to answer. We want to know whether there is an appropriate place for same-sex relationships within the context of a faithful relationship between two homosexually affected persons. It is clear that the Bible forbids many kinds of homosexual sins, like participating in a gang rape (whether homosexual or heterosexual), sexually abusing children, engaging in sexual acts as part of idol worship, or promiscuously giving in to every sexual desire. All these are clearly in violation of God's intention for sexuality. The Bible condemns these for heterosexuals and homosexuals. But that is not the controversial issue that Christians are debating. We are all in agreement that these things are contrary to God's will. But is there an appropriate place for homosexually affected persons to find sexual fulfillment in a stable and faithful partnership? That is the question on which Christian people disagree. The Bible does not address the issue, these interpreters say, at least not directly.

What are the implications of these two observations? Are we to conclude that homosexual relations within a faithful partnership are condemned along with all other forms of homosexual activity? Or are we to conclude that the Bible does not directly address the question we are asking? Bible interpreters are having a hard time reaching agreement. For now we leave the question open and continue our discussion of relevant biblical texts.

Third, the holiness code of the Old Testament includes the following: "You shall not lie with a male as with a woman; it is an abomination" (Leviticus 18:22), and "If a man lies with a male as with a woman, both of them have committed an abomination; they shall be put to death" (20:13). The labeling of acts as abominations and the penalty of death for them indicate the seriousness of this prohibition. For many interpreters, the Bible speaks plainly, and these texts unequivocally answer the question at hand. Other interpreters point out that the context of these prohibitions casts considerable doubt on this conclusion. The holiness code has as its goal the prohibition of practices that characterized pagan neighbors and their idol worship. Thus the text speaks to perverted worship, not perverted sexuality, and certainly not to faithful homosexual partnerships.

Israel was called to avoid the abominations associated with the ungodly nations around them (see Leviticus 18:1-5). Their pagan neighbors incorporated sexual, including homosexual, practices into the idol worship associated with their fertility cults. Indeed, the worshippers employed both male and female temple prostitutes.

If it is correct that the prohibitions of Leviticus 18:22 and 20:13 relate primarily to perverted worship, then the teaching of these texts would seem to be that sexuality is God's gift, but it represents a relationship between humans and not an avenue of connection to the divine world. Thus sexual experiences as a part of worship are both a misuse of sex and a misunderstanding of worship.

On this point the Old and New Testaments are in agreement. Visiting a temple prostitute is no innocent matter. It is a perversion of God's intentions (see also 1 Corinthians 6:15).

The crucial question for this discussion is whether the clear prohibitions of Leviticus are normative for all forms of same-sex relationship, even when they have nothing to do with worship. Does the Old Testament unequivocally forbid faithful homosexual partnerships along with whatever forms of homosexuality are clearly forbidden in this text. Interpreters are not in agreement.

Some maintain that Leviticus does not state the reason for its prohibitions, nor is there any need for it to do so. Forbidden is forbidden. God has reasons for the prohibition, whether or not we are told what they are. Now, that sounds very pious, but unfortunately the argument fails to persuade. After all, in the very same context—in fact, right between the two prohibitions cited above—we read the following: "You shall not sow your field with two kinds of seed; nor shall you put on a garment made of two different materials" (Leviticus 19:19). Which farmer would maintain that the first half of that verse represents a permanent prohibition? Which of us hold to the second half when we choose the clothes we wear? We do not consider Leviticus 19:19 a permanent prohibition, nor should we. It was related to the fertility practices of Israel's pagan neighbors and was to be avoided by them in that context for that reason. It is at least a fair question to ask whether the same might be true of the prohibitions in Leviticus 18:22 and 20:13. Moreover, by what right do we pick and choose which parts of a text to apply literally? Is it not sheer inconsistency to say that the prohibition of homosexual relationships stands, but the prescription of the death penalty for it does not?

Richard Hays is surely right when he says, "The church is faced with the task of discerning whether Israel's traditional norms remain in force for the new community of Jesus' followers. In order to see what decisions the early church made about this matter, we must turn to the New Testament."[8] It is beyond doubt that a very large number of commands and prohibitions in the holiness code have lost their relevance for Christians, at least for Gentiles (see especially Acts 15). Are the prohibitions of Leviticus 18:22 and 20:13 among them? Or is homosexuality in all its forms permanently prohibited by these verses? Or did this verse never intend to answer the key questions for which we seek answers?

Fourth, the Bible speaks often concerning the "sin of Sodom." Genesis 19:1-13 tells the horrifying story about the men of Sodom who tried to arrange the gang rape of the two angels who had come to visit the resident foreigner, Lot. Perhaps their intention was to demonstrate their contempt for these strangers. It is clear that if they had carried out their intentions, it would have been a homosexual act. It is equally clear that their intended behavior would have been wrong whether or not it involved homosexuality. A gang rape of any kind would have been a horrible sin, no less so if Lot's immoral offer of his virgin daughter as a substitute had led to a heterosexual gang rape. When the story is read as a whole and the references to it throughout Scripture are checked, we discover that this story helps us very little in finding an answer to the questions being discussed here.

- It is rather obvious that this is not a story about homosexually affected people. It would be preposterous to maintain that "the men of the city, the men of Sodom, both young and old, *all the people to the last man*" (Genesis 19:4, emphasis added) were homosexuals. In fact it is impossible to determine whether or not there were any among them who were homosexually affected. So this text is not about "what homosexuals do."
- The Bible never defines the "sin of Sodom" as homosexuality (see Isaiah 1:15-17; 3:9; Ezekiel 16:49; 2 Peter 2:6-10;

Jude 7; and fifteen other texts that mention Sodom). When the Old Testament refers to the sins of Sodom, it highlights social injustice, pride, and violating the rules of hospitality to strangers. In the New Testament, Sodom's sin is more explicitly sexual, but that is because it was a case of intended illicit sex between humans and divine beings, not because it was homosexual. Nowhere in Scripture is "the sin of Sodom" clearly identified as homosexuality, certainly not as homosexual partnerships, the topic under discussion here.

• The Genesis text clearly indicates that the men of Sodom were attempting to arrange a horribly sinful act. However, the text implies that this sin would have been violent sexual abuse, which is always sinful. Are homosexual relationships always sinful? That is the question under discussion. The story of Sodom, no doubt to the surprise of many, may not actually contribute much to the discussion.

• A somewhat similar yet even more horrifying story in Judges 19:2-26, in which a prophet's concubine is brutally gang raped, supports the claim that the primary issue here is sexual abuse, not homosexuality or heterosexuality.

• The two stories also illustrate what modern researchers are also saying: sexually abusive men are those least likely to care about the gender of their victims. They are abusing power by imposing their sexuality on another, and it seems to matter little whether their victim is male or female. At any rate, the majority of all men who sexually abuse young boys are not homosexuals but rather those boys' heterosexual fathers.

Fifth, several New Testament texts list various kinds of homosexual practices alongside other sins. Usually, the list specifies things that are done in the world of nonbelievers but must not be practiced by those who belong to God. For example, we read, "Do you not know that wrongdoers will not inherit the kingdom of God? Do not be deceived! Fornicators [*pornoi*], idolaters, adulterers, male prostitutes [*malachoi*], sodomites [*arsenokoitai*], thieves, the greedy, drunkards, revilers, robbers—none of these will inherit the kingdom of God" (1 Corinthians 6:9-10; see also 1 Timothy 1:10). But here we run into some translation difficulties. What exactly is *malachoi*? (male prostitutes? effeminate? homosexuals? the male who plays a "female role" in gay sex?) What is *arsenokoitai*? (homosexuals? the man who plays the "male role" in gay sex? sodomites?) The various ways these words are translated shows that there is at least uncertainty. It seems clear enough that some form of homosexual relationship is being referred to here as one of the many sins to be avoided. It is less clear that anyone reading the text in the first century would have thought it addressed a loving homosexual partnership, if they even imagined that such a thing was possible.

Sixth, many interpreters view Romans 1:26-27 as the clearest teaching on homosexuality:

> For this reason God gave them up to degrading passions. Their women exchanged natural intercourse for unnatural, and in the same way also the men, giving up natural intercourse with women, were consumed with passion for one another. Men committed shameless acts with men and received in their own persons the due penalty for their error.

It is clear from the context that Romans 1 was not designed primarily to address the issue of homosexuality. Rather, Paul shows what happens when people do not recognize God as God, and how that leads to perverting God's good intentions. Homosexual relations are used here as an illustration of the real point being made. Still, such relationships are here clearly discussed and, for the one and only time in all Scripture, female homosexuality is included. The core teaching of Paul here is that because humanity in general has not recognized God, has not appropriately worshipped God, God has delivered them over to perverted thoughts, worship, and behavior (for example in homosexual relationships). God's hand of judgment on sinful humankind is shown in the fact that God hands them over to forms of worship and lifestyle that are not part of God's good plan.

Paul does not say here that God's judgment falls on people who are homosexual. In that sense he reverses the cause-and-effect relationship. According to this text, moral perversion is the result, not the cause, of God's wrath. God's judgment falls and we see evidence of it in the fact that this world contains, among other things, distorted sexuality. The text also does not say that God's judgment has fallen on individual persons and as a result they themselves have become homosexual. Paul says no more and no less here than, in a fallen world, some people have given up "natural intercourse" in exchange for "unnatural."

Some suggest that Paul's point could be made just as well if cancer were used as an example. Cancer did not belong to life in the garden of Eden and will not be present in Paradise. It is part of what characterizes this fallen world. Its occurrence should not be interpreted as God's judgment on the individual who contracts it. Yet it is one of the clear signs that we live in a fallen world.

Yet the cancer comparison does not seem quite adequate. Paul goes on to list other things that characterize a fallen world and its people, and it is not a list of unavoidable diseases. It is a list of sins to be avoided, a list including such things as covetousness, envy, and strife (see vv. 29-31). These show that humans have not recognized and worshipped God properly.

Others suggest that this text ignores, or perhaps even deliberately excludes, persons who are homosexually affected. It speaks of those who, contrary to nature, have same-sex relationships. According to these interpreters, persons who are homosexually affected would experience heterosexual relationships as contrary to nature. For them a homosexual partnership is natural. The text does not address them and their sexuality. Moreover, Paul is clearly speaking of being "consumed with passion" (v. 27) and giving in to it. According to this argument, he is not discussing loving partnerships involving homosexually affected persons, and therefore this text does not help us answer the crucial question at hand.

Still others suggest that because the context is undeniably one of worship and its perverted forms, Paul is speaking of those homosexual practices that pagans included in their temple activities (see also the discussion of Leviticus 18:22 and 20:13 above). If that is Paul's only concern here, our question is again left unanswered by this text.

Yet many interpreters are convinced that this text speaks a clear word. Same-sex relationships are a perverted form of sex. People are tempted to commit many kinds of sins, and some are tempted to commit this kind. The presence of strong temptations and the fact that people give in to them is evidence of a fallen world under God's wrath. Yet even if we conclude that this text defines all homosexual relations as sinful, we have no right to consider them as something that is in principle worse than covetousness, envy, strife, and so on.

Seventh, homosexuality is either not addressed at all by Jesus or else only alluded to in Matthew 19:12. Here Jesus says, "For there are eunuchs who have been so from birth, and there are eunuchs who have been made eunuchs by others, and there are eunuchs who have made themselves eunuchs for the sake of the kingdom of heaven. Let anyone accept this who can." If in fact this verse was intended as a reference to homosexuality—that is, eunuchs by birth or because others made them so—it is clear that for Jesus the appropriate alternative for those "unable to marry" (as some translations word it) is not a homosexual partnership but rather celibacy, that is, choosing the eunuch option for the sake of God's kingdom.

Eighth, we are called to limit sexual expression to the boundaries of a heterosexual marriage. This is the conclusion we must reach if we hold that Genesis 1 and 2 are designed not only to define marriage but also to specify the only appropriate context for sexual relations: "Therefore a man leaves his father and his mother and clings to his wife, and they become one flesh" (Genesis 2:24). This also seems to be the assumption of many other biblical texts, including Matthew 5:27-28; 19:4-6, 12; 1 Corinthians 7; and Ephesians 5:21-23.

The Bottom Line

As we've seen, many claim that the Bible speaks clearly on the subject of homosexuality. A careful look at the biblical texts and their contexts, however, reveals that there is less clarity than some people want. That of course does not mean it is inappropriate to reach personal convictions about these things. It does mean, however, that we have no right to consider every other view to be clearly and self-evidently unbiblical and wrong. I have no right to assume that people who believe differently about this issue than I do are taking the Bible less seriously than I or that they are not being honest and sincere, or that they are not thinking as carefully. We read the Bible with different lenses and we often disagree. Moreover, we often approach biblical texts with somewhat different hermeneutical approaches and assumptions. That is to say, we build differently the bridge that connects the message of the Scriptures with the situations to which we want to apply it.

My personal estimate is that the first, sixth, and eighth points provide the best support for the view that same-sex sexual relationships are always outside God's plan for human sexuality. There are many ways to miss the mark when it comes to sexuality, and that is true both for heterosexuals and for homosexuals. But for heterosexuality, the Bible provides positive guidance, defining the appropriate contexts in which sexual activity is God-intended and good. For homosexuality there simply is no positive context or form defined in Scripture. Is that a coincidence or is the silence telling? It seems as though the Bible is saying that God's original plan for sex does not include sex acts in same-sex partnerships. That these occur and that many desire them is evidence that we live in a fallen world.

In order to have a healthy discussion of this issue, I think we would do ourselves a favor if we remained clear about some things and if we observed some appropriate ground rules for processing the question.

1. **We are talking about people whom God loves.** Though we are in search of truth and guidelines, though we aim to be objective and factual, we are still talking about real people whom God loves. It is difficult to avoid using pronouns like *we* for heterosexuals and *they* for homosexuals when in fact I am a heterosexual, as are most of my readers, and the sentences need to be grammatically correct. Yet if a discussion of this issue deteriorates to one of us and them, and if it implies that we are the norm and they are not, we easily find ourselves pushing away people whom God loves. We will no doubt also end up talking only *about* them and never *with* them. If we have no idea who the people are about whom we are talking, we might do well to first get to know some of them.

2. **One-sided arguments never promote a helpful discussion.** If we insist on quoting only the Bible interpreters and the scientists who support our view and then speak as though every alternative view is naïve, dishonest, or silly, we will not likely convince anyone.

3. **Unpersuasive claims undermine an argument.** I have heard people use arguments such as the following:

- The reason homosexuality is wrong is because it cannot lead to procreation.
- All Old Testament commands apply today just as they did for Israel.
- The situation that occasions a biblical prohibition is irrelevant to its meaning and its intended application.

- If someone finds something personally fulfilling, it is the right thing for that person.
- Everyone should be free to decide for themselves what they want to do.
- Homosexuals are usually sexually abusive.

The problem is that arguments like these are either false, unbiblical, inappropriately prejudicial, or simply cannot be followed through consistently. With such arguments, we provide no support for our conclusions and may even weaken otherwise good arguments.

4. **Honesty and consistency are valuable goods in this discussion.** We must all examine ourselves, whether we do not take biblical texts literally whenever they provide support for the conclusions we want to reach and reapply biblical texts when that is necessary in order to arrive at a desired conclusion. Our methods are often far from clean and clear.

5. **A basic course in biblical hermeneutics would be a great help.** If we are looking for "biblical" answers, it does not suffice to examine what the text says. We need to examine why it says what it says. We need to examine what other Scriptures contribute to the topic. And we need to ask what an appropriate application would be in a situation quite different from the one that occasioned the text in the first place.

6. **We are not being presumptuous if we hold to personal convictions about what constitutes sin.** I have heard people ask, "Who are you to presume to decide for someone else what is sin?" But that is not quite fair. If I am convinced that something is sin, I am not deciding what other people should avoid. That would indeed be presumptuous. Rather, I am reaching conclusions concerning what I believe God says about the matter. I have both the right and the responsibility to seek these conclusions, even while recognizing that others may well reach different conclusions.

7. In the face of so many unanswered questions, we need to be open-minded and patient with others. It is good to be convinced. But there is no room here for arrogance or stubbornness.

My Personal Convictions

I do not want my personal convictions about this topic to take center stage. The goal of this chapter has been to offer suggestions for a healthy discussion. But as I bring this chapter to its conclusion, I offer the conclusions that I presently hold on this important topic. I do this not to try to persuade readers to accept them, but for readers to consider where they agree and where they disagree and why.

My personal view is that sexual relationships between persons of the same sex do not correspond to God's intention for human sexuality. It is not a coincidence that God created humankind male and female. God planned it to be that way. The complementary and characteristic differences between male and female form the background to God's design for the one-flesh relationship. Further, God's intention is that sexual union occur within marriage. The only alternative, as the New Testament clearly presents, is sexual abstinence as a single person.

As I suggested earlier, the first, sixth, and eighth points discussed above seem most persuasive to me. The Bible uniformly speaks negatively of homosexual relationships; Romans 1 uses it as an example of behavior outside God's original design; Genesis 1 defines marriage as a union of a man and a woman. These three claims seem to me defensible and sufficient to point in a clear direction.

Those who reach similar conclusions often search for additional arguments to support their convictions, and a chain reaction often results: many would say that if I am persuaded by points 1, 6, and 8, then I can look for additional support by reexamining the other points. Thus I conclude that the prohibitions of Leviticus are not addressing cultic sexual practices but all forms of homosexuality. Similarly I conclude that the "sin of Sodom" did indeed include homosexuality and not merely rejecting foreigners. That in turn convinces me that the references to homosexual practices on the "sin lists" of the New Testament prove that all forms of homosexuality are always sin. Originally convinced by three arguments that seem decisive, they quickly add three more, declaring these also to be valid.

But a chain does not become stronger by adding more links to it. When we declare as valid arguments that others strongly suspect are invalid, we weaken rather than strengthen the biblical support for our conclusions. Thus I choose to restrict myself to points 1, 6, and 8 as the biblical basis for my perspective on homosexuality. These convince me that it is biblically inappropriate to view homosexuality as an appropriate alternative sexual lifestyle. God designed a marriage between a man and a woman to be the appropriate context for sexual intimacy and also the clearest human illustration for the complementarities that exist within the Godhead and between God and God's people.

As I observe churches that share my perspective on this issue, I am troubled by the inconsistency of our responses to sexual sin. Too often we take violations of God's standard very seriously when they are homosexual but silently ignore them if they are heterosexual.

But no matter what my view, no matter what your view, we will encounter fellow believers in our churches who have reached other conclusions. Because people have differing convictions about this topic, not only in society and in the scientific community but also among Bible interpreters and Christian churches, we need to practice open-heartedness, a merciful attitude, and a listening posture. Though we seek consensus, we should also be open to the possibility that it will be hard to reach. That means we need to live in harmony with those who believe differently than we do. I, for one, could participate fully in a congregation where not all members have reached the same conclusions as I have on this topic. Hays's warning here is apropos: "If the church is going to start practicing the discipline of exclusion from the community, there are other issues far more important than homosexuality where we should begin to draw a line in the dirt: violence and materialism, for example."[9]

In my view, we as Christians have not been commissioned by God to attempt to enshrine our understanding of Christian ethics into the law codes of our country. Those committed to Jesus, those who participate in his discipleship family, decide freely to follow Jesus. We do not depend on a police force and the threat of punishment to force us into compliance with God's standards. We do not depend on the state to pressure those around us who are not followers of Jesus to act as though they are.

So even if we were all in agreement that homosexual partnerships are outside God's will, I do not believe it is our responsibility to make or keep them illegal. On the contrary, while we support laws that protect people from being harmed by others, we also support laws that preserve human rights, even the right of non-Christians to act un-Christian. We are not called to use the civil law to make the world more Christian. Rather, our calling is to live in contrast to the ways of the world and thus to bear witness to the reality of God's kingdom. Our calling is to live in accordance with God's will, whether the laws of the land support us or not.

Discussion Questions

1. How do you explain the phenomenon that scientists, Bible interpreters, and "normal Christians" so often reach such widely diverging conclusions on the topic of homosexuality?

2. How do you respond to the author's claim that the Bible's teaching on this subject is not quite as clear as most people assume?

3. Do you personally know people who are homosexually affected? Does your contact with them influence you when

you seek to determine what is right and wrong on the subject? Should it?

For Further Reading

Grimsrud, Ted and Mark Thiessen Nation. *Reasoning Together: A Conversation on Homosexuality*. Scottdale, PA: Herald Press, 2008 (forthcoming).

Hays, Richard. *The Moral Vision of the New Testament*. San Francisco: Harper, 1996.

Stott, John. *Same-Sex Partnerships: A Christian Perspective*. Grand Rapids, MI: Revell, 1998.

Swartley, Willard M. *Homosexuality: Biblical Interpretation and Moral Discernment*. Scottdale, PA: Herald Press, 2003.

8

Money and Possessions

As Christians we confess that all we are and all we have belong to God. But what are the implications of saying that our money, resources, and influence are truly God's? How can we learn to serve God and not Mammon? This chapter provides tools for churches as they consider the appropriate applications of biblical teaching on this important topic.

A Dream

I dreamed that I was just settling into my easy chair to relax a little, and God was there. All around me were the visible signs of my comfortable life—evidences of God's blessing, I liked to call them. I was just about to express my gratitude for all the nice things around me when God stopped me with a startling question: "Which of the things you possess would you give me if I asked you for it?" I immediately tensed. What does God have in mind here? But then I looked around and quickly found many things I would be happy enough to do without and let God have if God wanted them. I set them out in the middle of my living room and was impressed with how many I had found so quickly.

I looked expectantly in God's direction. But God seemed to be waiting. Okay, I thought, I can find even more things I would be willing to relinquish, if God were to demand them of me. The pile in my living room grew as the shelves and the corners of my room began to look bare. I found more and more things I would be willing to do without if necessary. But still God waited. After a while I found it getting more and more difficult. I thought carefully about each object. Would I really be willing to do without this? And God waited.

I held my last treasure in my hand and struggled. Could I really give this up? In the end, I did not throw it on the pile. What I did instead was sneak it quickly under several other items, well out of sight, and hoped God hadn't noticed. The moment of truth had arrived.

"There you are, God," I said triumphantly. "Take whatever you want."

I hoped, of course, that God would smile at me and say, "Thanks. You passed the test with flying colors. I just wanted to know if you were willing. You can keep your things." But what if God instead responded, "Well done. I hoped you would be willing to give it all up. I'll take it then."

Well, God did neither. Instead God came nearer and carefully examined the pile. God walked around the pile and stopped right near the very last treasure that I had carefully hidden, and pointing toward my treasure, God said, "I think I will take only *that*!" And just as God was about to take hold of the piece I had so carefully sneaked into the pile, I cried out, "No, Lord, you really can have everything, just please not *that*."

God answered, "My child, I don't want to take everything away from you. I only want your *that*. I only want that which you want to withhold from me. Everything else belongs to me already."

&

I am continually amazed at how openly and often the Bible talks about money and how seldom and guardedly we do. Does the Scripture give us guidance for questions about money and possessions? Are the age-old biblical guidelines relevant at all in our complicated market economy? In this chapter I draw some basic principles from the Scriptures and then invite Christian communities to begin to dialogue about practicing what the Bible teaches.

Everything Belongs to God

What belongs to me really belongs to God. That is the basic biblical understanding of possessions, money, land, and everything that we gladly call our own. "The earth is the Lord's and all that is in it, the world, and those who live in it" (Psalm 24:1). "Heaven and the heaven of heavens belong to the Lord your God, the earth with all that is in it" (Deuteronomy 10:14). Two basic principles can be drawn from this biblical confession.

First, we are invited to receive and enjoy everything we have as God's good gifts to us. Our God is generous, and we, who are so well taken care of, are a thankful people. We honor God for the generous gifts we've been given. For example, Paul argued, "Eat whatever is sold in the meat market without raising any question on the ground of conscience, for 'the earth and its fullness are the Lord's'" (1 Corinthians 10:25-26). And, "Everything created by God is good, and nothing is to be rejected, provided it is received with thanksgiving" (1 Timothy 4:4). That is one side of the coin. God generously gives, so that all our needs are met and we have wonderful things to celebrate.

Second, we are God's stewards, charged to faithfully manage the things that belong to God. The Bible does not recognize the idea of completely private ownership. There is no area of our lives where we have the right to say to God, "You can have everything else, but not *that*." Whatever God blesses us with, it still belongs ultimately to God. So if God should ever say to us, "I've decided that I now want to give that to somebody else," we have no right to reply, "But you gave it to me; it's mine." C. S. Lewis once said, "Nothing that you have not given away will ever be really yours."[10]

Enjoying and Sharing

God has graciously and generously given to us. The Bible says that over and over again. If God takes care of the birds and the lilies, how much more will God care for us? We have no need to worry (see Matthew 6:25-34; Luke 12:7, 22-34).

Just as clearly the Bible says, "If we have food and clothing, we will be content with these" (1 Timothy 6:8). God does not "graciously give" all of us BMWs, luxury homes, and vacations in the Bahamas. In God's plan, those who have more than enough share with those who have too little. Paul argues that we need to aim for a fair balance: those who presently have too much share with those who are suffering (see 2 Corinthians 8:13-15). We have received much and we are called to share it generously.

Deuteronomy 15:11 spoke a clear word to Israel: "Since there will never cease to be some in need on the earth, I therefore command you, 'Open your hand to the poor and needy neighbor in your land.'" In the same context we read, "There will, however, be no one in need among you, because the Lord is sure to bless you in the land that the Lord your God is giving you as a possession to occupy, if only you will obey the Lord your God by diligently observing this entire commandment that I command you today" (15:4-5). The primary cause of poverty is not a lack of resources; it is that the world's resources are not fairly distributed. Israel in the Old Testament and the believing community in the New Testament hear God's primary plan for dealing with poverty: "Whoever gives to the poor will lack nothing" (Proverbs 28:27).

What is our typical response to all this? We say it is all oversimplified. The world is more complicated today than it was then. We need many things that were unnecessary earlier. We can't simply apply directly to our lives teachings that we read in the Old Testament. We can't even literally do everything the New Testament says. The Bible's instructions were given to people living in completely different circumstances than ours. If we really tried to apply all of the Bible's instructions about money directly and literally to our situation in a modern market economy, we would often find it to be completely impossible or utterly meaningless.

All of that is true. But that does not mean the Bible's instructions are useless and irrelevant. It means we need creative and generous people with common sense and receptive spirits to discern how we can in fact learn from Scripture and apply its basic teachings appropriately in the real world. I venture to propose that, if we do that, we will indeed find good guidance and a lot of helpful motivation to handle our money and possessions in ways that please God and accomplish God's purposes.

These two foundations—what belongs to us really belongs to God and what God graciously gives us we generously share—are clearly laid out for us in Scripture. But how do we build on that?

Old Testament Structures

God did not simply leave it up to the Israelites to figure out how to take these two basic principles and somehow put them into practice. Rather, God gave Israel a number of very specific structures designed to take these principles and regulate how they were enacted in life.

The tithe. If the New Testament frees us from the legal obligation to give the tithe—that is, a tenth of everything—the Old Testament certainly did not do that for the ancient Israelites. It was required of them, and the tithe was to be paid alongside other required contributions and taxes. Jesus criticized the legalism of the hypocrites who carefully paid their tithes on mint, dill, and cumin but in the process neglected the more important things—justice, mercy, and faithfulness (see Matthew 23:23). But he never suggested that the idea of the tithe was obsolete. Neither does any other text in the New Testament.

The truth is that Israel often practiced justice, mercy, and faithfulness precisely by giving their tithes. The money, the animals, and the grains that were given in the tithe were not used only to keep a religious system running. They were not used merely to decorate the temple's walls or buy new musical instruments. More frequently they were used for "the Levites, because they have no allotment or inheritance with you, as well as the resident aliens, the orphans, and the widows in your towns" (Deuteronomy 14:29). Those who had no harvest to draw on received the tithes and other gifts.

No-interest loans. For the Israelites who were reduced to poverty and needed to borrow money, the law said, "Do not take interest in advance or otherwise make a profit from them" (Leviticus 25:36). The basis for this prohibition was that both Israel's freedom and the land they owned were to be viewed as God's gifts. Israel would never be able to pay God back for all of God's gifts to them. How then can those who have money take advantage of the poor by profiting from the poorer person's misfortune?

The Sabbath. Six days each week were given to Israel to accomplish their work. All their days belonged to God, but the seventh one was to be sanctified and set apart for special, divinely ordained purposes. First and foremost, the day was set aside to honor the Creator, which meant that Israel also had to trust the Creator to provide what they needed in six days. God did that, for example, by sending double the normal amount of manna in the wilderness just in time for the Sabbath. The Sabbath also meant rest for work animals and farm workers so that no one would be worked to death. It would also prevent people from becoming workaholics. The seventh day created space to be invested in weekly worship and fellowship experiences in the community of believers. The way Jesus used the Sabbath also created opportunities to do good to others. By setting aside the seventh day, we are symbolizing and celebrating that all our days belong to God. We express that anew each week as we keep the Sabbath.

The sabbath year. God not only gave Israel sufficient provision in six days to serve their needs all week, God also gave Israel enough in the sixth year to carry them through the seventh. For that reason Israel was to let the land lie fallow every seven years: "It shall be a year of complete rest for the land" (Leviticus 25:5). Not only that. If someone had become poor and had accumulated so many debts that he could survive only as an indentured servant, in the seventh year he was granted his freedom and forgiveness of his debts (see Exodus 21:2). The inequities of life were to be overcome through debt forgiveness and amnesty. People were regularly given the chance to start over. That is what the Bible calls justice. We might be inclined to call it mercy, but God says that we owe new beginnings to each other. After all, everything we are and have has been given to us freely by God.

The jubilee year. The most radical new beginning was supposed to take place every fifty years. Leviticus 25 describes the radical changes that were to be introduced by the blowing of the trumpet on the day of atonement every jubilee year (see v. 9); "And you shall hallow the fiftieth year and you shall proclaim liberty throughout the land to all its inhabitants. It shall be a jubilee for you: you shall return, every one of you, to your property and every one of you to your family" (v. 10). All servants who had debts to their masters were to be set free and all debts canceled. The land that had been collected by the wealthier members of the community was to be given back to its original owners, just like that! The economic and social conditions were to be leveled again, everything divided up again, fair and square.

We can hardly hear instructions like that. "Unfair," we'd say. "That belongs to me. I earned it, and justly too." But God saw things very differently. As for the land: "The land shall not be sold in perpetuity, for the land is mine; with me you are but aliens and tenants" (v. 23). As for the servants: "For they are my servants, whom I brought out of the land of Egypt; they shall not be sold as slaves are sold" (v. 42). God is the one who delivered Israel and entrusted them with the land, each family with a fair share. If God now chooses to redistribute the land once more, well, that is up to God. We are only stewards, taking care of the land on God's behalf.

There is no evidence anywhere in Scripture that Israel ever practiced the Jubilee. But that changes nothing in terms of the basic principles this institution reveals concerning God's intention for God's own property and for God's own people. We see this clearly in the fact that the prophet Isaiah picked up the concept (not the legal requirement!) of jubilee and turned it into an eschatological principle. He prophesied that with the coming of the Messiah and God's kingdom, the true jubilee would become a reality (see Isaiah 61:1-3).

Jesus chose jubilee as a central symbol for his ministry, quoting Isaiah's prophecy and saying, "Today this scripture has been fulfilled in your hearing" (Luke 4:21). Jesus in no way attempted to take land from anyone and give it to someone else. Nor did he tear up anyone's loan papers. But the principles of generous sharing, especially with those lacking resources and status, were principles he embodied in his ministry and in his teaching. We who belong to this kingdom that Jesus inaugurated are called to do the same.

A Few Probes into the New Testament

Even to touch briefly on all the New Testament teaching concerning wealth and property would take far more room than is available here. Jesus spoke more often about money than he did about heaven. Luke's Gospel especially has an emphasis on the attitudes of faithful disciples toward their possessions and the poor people around them. One need only examine a whole host of parables about money in Luke. Through them Jesus taught, among other things,

- that God's generosity is the basis for our generous sharing with each other;

- that God will forgive and receive back even those who squander God's resources;
- that God's forgiveness of our debts should motivate us to forgive those indebted to us;
- that we are to be good stewards, investing wisely and courageously what God has entrusted to us;
- that selfish hoarding of possessions puts us in danger of God's judgment;
- that the teachings of Moses and the prophets on the topic of possessions are still valid.

In addition to parables, the Gospels contain numerous narratives that teach us to show generosity to others who have less than we do and to trust God to meet our needs.

"How hard it is for those who have wealth to enter the kingdom of God!" (Luke 18:24). These words astonished Jesus' disciples. But over and over Jesus' statement has proven itself true. In the larger context, Jesus seems to be saying it is actually impossible for anybody to enter into the kingdom of God—and for rich people even harder. His point is that participation in God's kingdom can be granted only as a gift; the right to it can never be earned. But it is especially difficult for those who are rich to open their hands and receive that gift, especially when they become aware as citizens of the kingdom that God will be the one who decides what they should do with their wealth. As citizens in God's kingdom we are but stewards of God's possessions. If God wants it all given to the poor, we have no basis on which to say no.

In the book of Acts we find that, in the early church, members freely shared their possessions, and everyone was given as much as they needed: "Now the whole group of those who believed were of one heart and mind, and no one claimed private ownership of any possessions, but everything they owned was held in common. . . . There was not a needy person among them, for as many as owned lands or houses sold them and brought the proceeds of what was sold" (Acts 4:32, 34). That is what they called *koinonia*, mutual participation in one another's lives.

Then there are the texts in which Paul speaks of the offering he was gathering for the Jerusalem believers (see especially 2 Corinthians 8:6-15). These texts show clearly how we are to think about money, excess, and the poverty of others. They show us that right thoughts lead to generous action. According to Paul, giving to others provides a valid test of the sincerity of people's love (see 8:8; also 1 John 3:17). He viewed it as an obligation, though not a legal requirement. It is an opportunity to build fellowship; it is a way of practicing justice, mercy, and faithfulness, the very things Jesus said represent the heart of God's law (see Matthew 23:23).

The World Today

A great deal has changed since Old Testament times, when the people of God were both a faith community and a nation. There was no clear distinction between the tithe and taxes—both were required. Whether the money and goods collected went for religious purposes or social purposes was not always easy to distinguish. By New Testament times, some of the Old Testament institutions had fallen by the wayside. Others were still practiced, but had become voluntary. Because they were voluntary, Paul had to appeal to the churches for help. In our day we expect social programs and tax rebates to contribute at least some toward helping those with fewer resources. The early church could count on neither of these.

Moreover, one can easily see that most of the Old Testament institutions assumed a farming economy, and direct application would work for hardly anybody today. But even farmers might well protest that the Old Testament teachings are impractical. It all depends on climate conditions, optimal crop rotations, types of soil, market demands, and many other factors. How relevant is the prohibition against charging interest when it is not the poor who are borrowing but rather those running large businesses or building expensive homes? In a market economy, where a certain level of inflation is anticipated, interest-free loans have a different meaning than they did in an economy where products were mostly traded.

Add to that other considerations. In biblical times people would have had neither the know-how nor the capacity to damage the environment, at least not nearly to the extent of today. When would it be our duty to make economic decisions that might hurt our bottom line but contribute to cleaner air and preserving the ozone layer? The Bible never contemplates or addresses questions like that. Nor did people back then ever scratch their heads wondering whether buying a product might contribute to unemployment or slave labor on the other side of the globe. Today these are all relevant considerations.

Precisely because so much has changed, the basic question needs to be asked: how can we take the biblical teaching seriously and apply it helpfully in our world? The starting point is a willingness to begin talking about money and its use. Bible interpreters need significant help from those who understand global economies, or we will find ourselves applying texts in all the wrong ways. Business owners need help from those who can work out biblical principles so that they don't too easily assume that whatever makes economic sense must also be the right thing to do. We all need one another so that we can look with integrity at these texts and apply them. If we help each other, we can discern guidelines that can be translated into wise decisions, and we will move from the Scriptures to real life. We will learn both to think and to act biblically in the ways we earn and spend, buy and sell, save and share.

Sometimes the tough questions we need to discuss will not be merely about money. Sometimes they involve the things money can buy: time, power, luxury goods. Are there some things we should choose to boycott? Maybe certain kinds of stocks, luxury items, or products that harm the natural environment? We will need to build a hermeneutical bridge that connects the world of Scripture and the world in which we live.

For that we need to learn to be more open with each other. Why would it be so bad if the members of my home fellowship group knew how much I earn, which financial decisions I am struggling with, where I could use good advice about a prospective purchase? Would it not be good if they knew where I am easily tempted? Do I find it hard to trust God to meet my needs? Am I tempted to make money dishonestly or to cheat on my taxes? Am I addicted to work? Is my financial portfolio my *that*, which I want to keep from God? How can we help each other in these matters if we all keep them secret?

Living Differently from the World

Paul wrote, "I appeal to you therefore, brothers and sisters, by the mercies of God, to present your bodies as a living sacrifice, holy and acceptable to God, which is your spiritual worship. Do not be conformed to this world, but be transformed by the renewing of your minds, so that you may discern what is the will of God—what is good and acceptable and perfect" (Romans 12:1-2). He is saying clearly that our life is our response to the grace of God. Part of that response involves answering God's grace with our money, possessions, time, influence, and opportunities. The text also clearly says that self-sacrificial living pleases God more than religious ceremonies. We can visit a thousand church services, but if Jesus is not Lord of our wallets, then God is probably less impressed with our church attendance than we suppose. Paul also makes clear here that there should be a noticeable difference between us and the world. We will think differently and we will act differently. That of course applies to money matters no less than to any other area. In every area of life, including this one, it is important to recognize the will of God. How can we work through all this in the mutually accountable community of Jesus-followers that we want to be?

I have some proposals regarding how we can work at these issues in church contexts. I have tried out these ideas with several groups and see a great deal of potential in them.

To start with, we work through the material I have presented above, reading and discussing both the topics and the texts cited there. While looking at the texts, participants can already begin to consider what kinds of principles are being promoted in them and some possibilities for applying those principles in our world.

After that, working groups are created, each one taking on a certain "personality" (see below) and covering a different aspect of the larger issue. After taking sufficient time to work through the questions, the groups gather again and discuss their findings and proposals. Here are the suggested groups and their respective study questions. Each group can formulate additional questions that seem important to them after studying the biblical material.

Group 1: I'm a businessperson (for self-employed people, people in business, farmers, and the like).

- Earn as much as possible, so that you will have more with which you can be generous. How do you evaluate this principle?
- When it comes to ethical business practices, what are some of the gray areas?
- How should a Christian way of treating employees be different from the way they are typically treated in our society?
- Should we as Christians, if we live according to the principles taught in Scripture, count on being economically less "successful" than the world?

Group 2: I'd like to help where I can (for those who want to contribute to a more just world in which resources are more fairly distributed).

- What are the most acute situations in our country and in other parts of the world where help is desperately needed right now?
- What kinds of attitudes and actions will help us to be part of the solution to economic disparity, rather than being a part of the problem?
- How can we and our congregation best learn to adopt these attitudes and actions?
- Which organizations can help us with this?

Group 3: I want to learn to shop according to Christian principles (for those who love to go shopping or most often do it for their families).

- What speaks against buying luxury goods? What are luxury goods anyway? (For me? For other people?)
- How much more should we be willing to pay in order to buy environmentally friendly goods? (What kinds of goods are those?)
- If we are seriously concerned about contributing to a fair distribution of the world's resources, how will that affect what we choose to buy or not buy?
- How can we enjoy God's good gifts to us without having a guilty conscience about them?

Group 4: "I want to help foster koinonia in our congregation" (for those who want that and are willing to put effort into making it happen).

- What is already happening in our congregation that helps to bring about a "fair balance" (2 Corinthians 8:13) between those who have abundance and those who have needs?
- Which good or bad experiences have I had in these matters?
- How do the things we can contribute relate to what govern-

ment programs try to accomplish in fostering economic justice?

- What concrete suggestions would we like to bring to the church to encourage all of us to grow in living generously and faithfully with our possessions?

Concluding True Story

When I left seminary and entered a church ministry, like most students, I had little money. I soon discovered that the church I entered had a very different attitude about possessions and money than I was accustomed to. I immediately experienced generous sharing and a surprising openness to talk about financial issues. In that time and place—1978, Ft. McMurray, Alberta—there was hardly any other affordable housing besides a mobile home on a rented lot. I did not have the two thousand dollars for the minimum down payment, but my brother did.

He came to me with a check in hand and said, "It's yours to buy your house. Pay it back whenever you can afford to do so, but not to me! Give the money under the same conditions to somebody else who needs it."

I bought my mobile home and within six months had saved enough that I could pass on the two thousand dollars to someone who also bought a mobile home. Then he passed along the money. Somewhere I completely lost track, but perhaps the money is still being passed on. Whatever may have happened to the original two thousand dollars, I can testify that it has been bearing interest in my life for three decades already. And I believe that the new attitudes I learned toward money and generous sharing through this experience are still bearing rich fruit in my life and in the lives of who knows how many other people. God knows!

Discussion Questions

1. What is my *that*—that which I am not very willing to

put at God's disposal, that which does not yet truly belong to God?

2. Which of the Old Testament institutions designed by God to contribute to creating just economic relationships and a leveling of social-economic disparities can we still practice today if we seek to apply them appropriately to our own cultural and economic systems?

3. What are some good experiences we have had with financial generosity that still bear rich fruit in our own lives?

For Further Reading

Halteman, James. *The Clashing Worlds of Economics and Faith.* Scottdale, PA: Herald Press, 1995.

Hussein, Bedru and Lynn Miller. *Stewardship for All: Two Believers Speak.* Intercourse, PA: Good Books, 2007.

Sider, Ronald J. *Rich Christians in an Age of Hunger: Moving from Affluence to Generosity.* Dallas: Word, 1997.

Part 3
Attitudes

We have now considered a variety of ethical issues. Sometimes you will have agreed with me, sometimes not. But I hope you will be better equipped to discuss these and other matters with fellow believers in ways that shed light rather than merely generate heat. Undoubtedly you will encounter people, even within your own Christian communities, who continue to disagree.

The challenge for us is to become the kind of Christian communities that can face disagreements head-on and find a way forward. The challenge of recognizing sin in ourselves and in others and throwing ourselves on the mercy of our heavenly Father confronts us. We face the challenge of being grace-givers who are so overwhelmed with God's grace to us that we seek to pass it on to those around us.

In the final section of this book I hope to inspire us to work at becoming that kind of church and those kinds of Christians. I examine a narrative about the early church, a parable of Jesus, and an incident in his life. All three texts have the power to challenge us and inspire us, and my prayer is that they will do so.

9

'It Has Seemed Good to the Holy Spirit'

The early church was also confronted with difficult questions, and in its history we can find insight regarding community decision making. How were they able to preserve unity and say, "It has seemed good to the Holy Spirit and to us" (Acts 15:28)? A set of guidelines drawn from Acts 15 can guide us with today's difficult questions.

Churches are often confronted with tough situations and agonizing decisions. Opinions and preferences clash. Feelings are aroused. Conflict emerges. The challenges of decision making far exceed our capacity to deal constructively with them. We discuss, sometimes we fight, and often we fail to reach consensus. We leave the discussions frustrated and discouraged. Or we somehow decide something, but we're not convinced. So afterward there is grumbling, or perhaps we go and do whatever we want anyway. The early church faced similar challenges, and the book of Acts provides glimpses of how they dealt with the challenges—sometimes well, sometimes not so well.

Things started out gloriously for the early church. Luke gives us glowing reports of their joy, their generosity, and their unity (see Acts 2:42-47; 4:34-37). But things soon became complicated. There were scandals, theological controversies, conflicts among

187

leading personalities. People with diverse backgrounds joined the growing church. As the gospel spread, the church discovered it was no small challenge to preserve unity.

The early church did not let the challenges overwhelm them. They learned to be flexible. They worked hard to discover what were central and unchanging components of the gospel and what needed to be adjusted to fit new situations. They trusted God's Spirit, studied the Scriptures, listened again to Jesus' words, and held fast to the core of the gospel. They discerned together what it meant for Jesus to be their Lord; they observed God at work among them; they were committed to follow God's will, whatever the cost. They were willing to be out of step with their culture and their world, clarifying more than once that their highest duty was to obey God, not to yield to the demands of earthly powers. Those who observed them could tell they had been with Jesus.

Then came perhaps the biggest challenge they had ever faced, one that seriously threatened to split the young church. Acts 15 describes the church's response to this major challenge. Through it all, the early Christians preserved their unity and reached consensus. It did not happen without significant negotiations. There were hefty discussions, serious disputes, and strong emotions, but in the end they reached a Spirit-inspired agreement. How did they manage it? Let's observe them and learn.

The Situation

For some time, the church in Antioch had been more progressive, more evangelistic, and more ready to experiment with new ideas than its counterpart in Jerusalem (see Acts 11:19-30; 13:1-3; 14:26-28). In fact, the Christians in Jerusalem, some of whom had a Pharisaic background, were intent on preserving their Jewish heritage. They were horrified when they learned that the Antiochian church was drawing Gentile converts directly out of paganism without demanding that they follow Jewish laws and traditions. They sent a delegation to Antioch. "And after Paul and Barnabas had no small dissension and debate with them, Paul and Barnabas and some of the others were appointed to go up to Jerusalem to discuss this question with the apostles and the elders" (Acts 15:2).

A storm front developed as two views collided. On one side, the Jewish teachers from Jerusalem represented the viewpoint of the "conservative" Jews. They were certain that Gentiles can indeed become Christians but only if they become Jews first. There is only one way to come to faith in Jesus. All must come through the same gate, the law of Israel and its fulfillment in Jesus.

On the other side, Paul and Barnabas defended the "progressive" church in Antioch. Many of the Christians in Antioch had been driven out of Jerusalem by persecution (see 11:19)—driven out, in fact, by conservative Jews. Maybe there were still some old injuries festering. This group was certain that God was at work leading Gentiles to faith in Jesus. The church must accept everyone God was bringing to faith. After all, Jesus had welcomed even tax collectors and sinners. According to Paul and Barnabas, a great deal was at stake in this dispute. If the church required Gentiles to accept the traditions of the Jews, they would be abandoning the core of the gospel. A conference was convened in Jerusalem to deal with the issues.

Issues of the Jerusalem Council

So, what was the conference all about, and what can we take from it?

The conference faced a significant theological decision. Under which conditions can a person come into a reconciled relationship with God? The question was in fact quite concrete: do Gentiles need to be circumcised? (see Acts 15:1). Circumcision was one of the rites through which Gentiles became full Jews. So behind the question of circumcision was the more basic one: do Gentiles have to become Jews to become Christians?

It was about the ethical implications of the answer to the first question. Along with submitting to circumcision, a proselyte to Judaism would also be obligated to follow the entire Law of Moses. Major ethical implications would follow if Gentiles were required to be circumcised.

It was about the ethnic implications of the larger issue. If Gentiles would not be required to adopt Jewish law, the church would be deciding that Jewish practices were not ethical issues at all but merely ethnic peculiarities. It would mean that Jewish practices were no longer essential elements of Christian faith and life.

It was about the practical implications of the Jew-Gentile question. If the unity of the church was to be preserved, there would have to be some give-and-take on both sides. They would need to be able to make compromises on some issues of Christian lifestyle. If conservative Jews were to dictate the terms of an agreement, many Gentiles would be driven out of the church. If the Gentiles dictated the terms, it would be impossible for conservative Jews to practice fellowship with these newcomers (see discussion of vv. 19-21 below).

It was about the means by which they reached a consensus. If the process was not a central concern at the conference, it surely was for the author of the text. It seems clear that Luke highlights their decision-making procedures so that future generations of Christians can find guidance when we find ourselves embroiled in seemingly insoluble conflict situations?

The Results of the Conference

The theological question. To clarify the theological issue, they determined, ironically enough, that the Pharisaic Christians had been both right and wrong. They had correctly insisted that there could be only one doorway to salvation; every person joining the church of Jesus Christ comes through the same door. But what was that one way? Here they had been mistaken. The doorway was not Judaism—not even for Jews! No one can be saved simply by living according to Jewish law. The doorway to salvation is the grace of the Lord Jesus. Thus they also gained clarity: Gentiles do not have to be circumcised; they do not have to proselytize; they do not have to obligate themselves to the entire Law of Moses. Peter explained: "On the contrary, we believe that we will be saved through the grace of the Lord Jesus, just as they will" (v. 11). Do we notice what happened? The Jews learned more about their own access to God's saving work through the experience of the Gentiles. Now they could see that their own salvation was not linked to the fact that they were Jews, to their circumcision or to their commitment to the Mosaic law. It was now clear to them that not only Gentile salvation, but also their own salvation, was linked to the grace God had given through the Lord Jesus. That's how both Jews and Gentiles are saved. There is only one way.

The ethical question. But what does that all mean? Can the Gentiles then throw out the whole Mosaic law and all its requirements? Is it not valid for them at all? What about the Jews? Is it not valid for them any longer either? Here we come to a significant difficulty in interpreting Acts 15.

How are we to interpret the four conditions named: "We should write to them to abstain only from things polluted by idols and from fornication and from whatever has been strangled and from blood" (v. 20; see also v. 29).

One problem is that there are various other possible translations for some of the terms. A related challenge is to determine what underlying principle explains the choice of these particular guidelines. On the surface it sounds as though these are being presented as the most significant issues addressed by the law, that the Gentiles are not required to observe all the details of the law, but the most important prohibitions of the law should indeed be taken seriously. But this of course does not work at all. Are we supposed to believe that eating a strangled animal is a more serious matter than lying, stealing, or killing? Were these things to be allowed for the Gentiles? Certainly not.

Some translations use marginal comments, bracketed words, or footnotes to alert readers to various difficulties with the text. One relates to the meaning of the word sometimes translated *fornication*. Another makes the doubtful suggestion that Old Testament guidelines for "foreigners among the Israelites" is in the background.

Without detailed argument, here are my views concerning the primary goals this list of four prohibitions was designed to accomplish. I suspect the council was aiming to do the following:

1. Make it not too difficult for the Gentiles (see v. 19). That's why they did not put ten or twenty things on the list.
2. Make it not too difficult for the Jews, either. To facilitate fellowship with Jews, the Gentiles had to be willing to forego some of the things that would be significant stumbling blocks for Jews (see v. 21).
3. Protect the new converts from slipping back into their old lifestyles. Some of the things on the list involved actions associated with their former idol worship. Continuing to do these things would make it easier for them to fall back into old religious and ethical practices incompatible with Christian faith.
4. Facilitate evangelism among both Gentiles and Jews. No doubt one side argued that they would never win Gentiles to faith if they have to start obeying hundreds of new laws. And the other side argued that they would never win more Jews if they have to associate with people who do everything we have always considered forbidden. Moreover, when Christians, both Jew and Gentile, are willing to restrict personal freedoms for the benefit of others, when the unity of the church weighs more heavily than personal preference, the church gains credibility. Others will be drawn to Christ

and the church when they observe what the power of the gospel can do.

The list of the four conditions for Gentile inclusion in the church appears in some translations to contain three matters of Jewish ceremonial law and one—fornication—that is an ethical matter. But the list makes far more sense if we view even that fourth one as a non-ethical matter.

The Greek word *porneia* sometimes means sexual sin generally, sometimes may specifically mean fornication. Here, however, it likely refers to marrying within forbidden degrees of affinity and consanguinity (in other words, marrying people to whom you are related, whether through blood or marriage), which was forbidden by Jews but not necessarily by other ethnic groups. If that is what porneia means here, all four elements on the list represent actions that are best avoided under certain circumstances but that are not necessarily sinful in other contexts. Put another way: none of the four conditions is a strictly ethical matter. All are matters that can be negotiated.

I believe that this short list makes no attempt at all to establish basic and permanent ethical guidelines. It would be far too incomplete to be a list of ethical requirements, even if porneia were translated as fornication. The Ten Commandments, for example, are conspicuously missing, commandments that the New Testament clearly presents as binding for all Christians—Jew and Gentile.

The list makes most sense if we view it as a negotiated list designed to accomplish the goals I suggested above. Nonnegotiable ethical matters—actions that are at all times and in all places sinful—are thus not addressed at all by this short list. The silent assumption of the entire New Testament is that an ethical lifestyle, lived according to the principles of God's kingdom and the norms of Christian discipleship, is expected of all Christians, whether Jew or Gentile. Nowhere in ethical instruction of the New Testament do we find comments as to whether ethical guidelines apply to

Jews or Gentiles or both. Though we may struggle to determine exactly what that ethical life should look like, we will get no help from this short list. It was not designed to define that.

The ethnic question. The Jewish Christians, especially the conservative Pharisaic ones in Jerusalem, were clearly being shown that issues they had always seen as ethical matters were in fact ethnic matters. Whether someone is circumcised, whether someone holds to the food laws of the Old Testament, whether various cleansing ceremonies were practiced, these are now clarified as non-ethical issues; they are ethnic issues only. As a result, the Jerusalem council clarified that ethnic diversity is acceptable and desirable within the church. Christians will and may live differently. We are thereby cautioned against seeing ethnic peculiarities as matters of ethics and especially against treating ethnic peculiarities as necessities for salvation.

We are reconciled to God through a relationship with Jesus made possible by God's grace. We learn along with other believers what an ethical Christian lifestyle involves. Most other things are ethnic, cultural, optional. That means we worship God and practice our Christian faith in diverse ways, and we relate to our surrounding culture in varying ways. But we must be willing to restrict our personal freedoms if that helps facilitate Christian fellowship or the witness of the church in the world. Above all we accept each other in Christ, as diverse as we are.

The practical question. The church was ready to adopt practical solutions to its problems, solutions that facilitated fellowship, Christian maturity, and witness. I suspect it was not easy to negotiate the four things to put on the list. Perhaps some wanted seven and others wanted only two. They ended up selecting four on which compromise was appropriate and that could facilitate the intended goals. The participants at the conference understood the choice of these four things as dictated by the needs of the moment and therefore as renegotiable in other circumstances. Not ten years later Paul was directly asked about one of these four issues. Is it always wrong to eat meat that has been sacrificed to idols? He answered that it depends on the circumstances (see 1 Corinthians 8:9-11; 10:23-33).

Paul understood the principles that lay behind the restrictions agreed on in Jerusalem, and he preserved these principles but proposed new applications when the situation changed. His approach should guide us as well. In every time and place we are challenged to discern how we can make it easier and not harder for newcomers to join the Christian community. Which restrictions are necessary so that the more conservative among us are not pushed too far? What guidelines will help new converts avoid slipping back into their pre-Christian lifestyles? What helps the church to gain a credible testimony? If our list of restrictions contains twenty elements, we will no doubt have erred on one side. If we are never willing or able to reach decisions that all can support, decisions that serve the church and its mission, then we err on the other side.

How Did They Manage All That?

Now that we have examined the results of the Jerusalem council, let's look briefly at the strategies they used to achieve them. Is there anything we can learn from the way they went about seeking solutions for their problems? I suggest the following points:

They came together, even if it cost a great deal of time and energy. It was at least a three-day trip from Antioch to Jerusalem. But the unity of the church was worth the effort expended. Sometimes a church can waste a great deal of time and dissipate a great deal of energy talking and debating when each member feels that it is important to argue their viewpoint. But the opposite is also true. Sometimes we cannot afford to break off the conversation until we have learned to talk openly and honestly with each other, to listen carefully and sympathetically to each other, to seek God's guidance together, and to find the clarity and unity that God wants to give us.

Everyone was given an opportunity to contribute to the discussion. Though the apostles and elders played a leading role, there are several indications in the text that everyone was given opportunity to participate (see Acts 15:4, 12). The text says that the whole assembly "kept silent." The Greek expression implies that before this they had spoken their mind, but they were now persuaded. If in our discussions only particularly gifted speakers dare to express their opinions, we need to work out procedures and develop a climate in which all the others are also able and willing to participate.

They recalled what God had done among them in the past. They were convinced they could learn something of God's will by observing how God had worked in their history: "You know that in the early days God made a choice among you, that I should be the one through whom the Gentiles would hear the message of the good news and become believers" (v. 7). For us this means that our church traditions are important and are not to be carelessly abandoned. God was at work in the past and led us to previous insights and decisions.

They recognized that God was now doing something new. "They told of all the signs and wonders that God had done through them among the Gentiles" (v. 12). That is the other side. Our traditions should never hold us prisoner and exclude new things God may be doing. We recognize that we did not understand the full truth in the past; that, in turn, helps us guard against thinking our present convictions constitute the full and final truth.

They examined the Scriptures. "This agrees with the words of the prophets," notes James in verse 15. We can seriously misunderstand God's activities in the past and present if we do not carefully examine the Scriptures. The Bible entered their discussion rather late in the process. For us it must come far earlier. The difference is that we already have the New Testament, whereas they relied heavily on the apostles who later wrote New Testament books. In that sense, when we examine the Scriptures, we have, as it were, the apostles present with us as well.

They aimed to make it easier and not harder for newcomers (see vv. 19-20). That should be our priority as well. Later in Paul's writings we see that he expected church members to be ready to make significant concessions for the sake of others, to limit their personal freedom for the benefit of the body. But he expected that not from the newcomers; he expected it from those already more mature in the faith. In fact, it is a sign of maturity when those who have been in the church for a long time are willing to smooth the path for newcomers and not expect them to make the major concessions.

They took seriously the interests of both sides in the debate. That, again, is the other side. The newcomers were also expected to make some concessions, to be willing to restrict their freedoms for the sake of those who had been in the church before they were. That is how true fellowship works. It seeks solutions that draw us closer together. Afterward we do not say, "You win; I lose." Nor do we say, "If I can't win; you shouldn't either." Instead we seek win-win solutions. If we can learn to concede to one another, we all win a wonderful fellowship that holds us and draws in others. If we gain that, we have lost nothing, even if a decision did not go the way we had wished, even if we need to restrict our personal freedoms.

They did not say, "It has seemed good to the Holy Spirit and to us," until they had reached consensus. Of course we want to invite the Holy Spirit to be present in our conversations. But if each one seeks to draw the Spirit onto his or her side ("It seems good to the Holy Spirit and to *me*"), we are not following the example of the early church. In fact I sometimes wonder how they knew that the decision they made corresponded to the leading of the Spirit. I suspect they knew precisely because they had reached consensus about it. They had taken the appropriate steps in seeking God's will. They had listened to each other; they had examined the Scriptures; they had recognized God at work; they had been willing to move courageously in new directions. They paved the way for others to come to faith and to join the fellowship. They agreed together. What else could this mean but that the Holy Spirit had been among them all along, leading to the right decision? How else could they interpret the results but to say that Jesus had kept his promise? When we act in his name and under his commission, he is with us, to the end of the age.

Conclusion

I am not sure whether Luke is just trying to be realistic or whether he had a sense of humor. At any rate, he does surprise us, I suspect, when we observe what he reports next in his narrative of the early church. Right after the encouraging story of a conflicted church preserving unity and finding God's will, Luke tells us that Paul and Barnabas were unable to resolve a conflict between them. These two, who had planted churches together, who had been co-workers in Antioch, who had just stood side by side for the truth of the gospel, now find themselves unable to settle their own dispute (see vv. 36-41). Their conflict escalates to the point that they go their separate ways, no longer able to preach the gospel together. As far as we know, they never ministered together again.

We are always human. We do not always achieve the unity we seek. But amazingly even the inability of Paul and Barnabas to find a common way became something God could use. They separated because they could not agree on who should join them for their next missionary journey. So two mission teams came into being, and the mission went on.

Perhaps if the success of the early church at the Jerusalem council intimidates us because we think it never works that well when we try it, we can take courage from the way Acts 15 ends. These early Christians were human too, and sometimes they failed. But God remained faithful, and God remains faithful when we fail. On the discipleship road we fail; we take detours; we go separate ways. But then we go on with the mission, and God does great things among us again.

Discussion Questions

1. Which are the questions that demand of us a clear yes or no in order to preserve the unity of the church on crucial foundational matters?

2. What are some issues on which the unity of the church is more effectively preserved by not demanding that all members believe or act in the same way?

3. Which of the eight final points presented in this chapter can help us most when we are aiming to reach consensus on crucial questions?

For Further Reading

Green, Michael. *I Believe in the Holy Spirit*. Grand Rapids, MI: Eerdmans, 2004.

Johnson, Luke Timothy. *Scripture and Discernment: Decision Making in the Church*. Nashville, TN: Abingdon Press, 1996.

McBride, Alfred. *The Gospel of the Holy Spirit*. New York: Hawthorn Books, 1975.

10

Two Sons and a Running Father

In the well-known parable of the prodigal son (Luke 15:11-32), Jesus reveals to us God's highest priority: relationships. Jesus shows us how far God is willing to go to rebuild relationships that have broken down. This impressive parable will occupy us in this chapter.

Story Time

One day Jesus was enjoying a party as he did often, especially when there were lots of sinners around. In Jesus' day, these people were a lot more fun to be with than religious people. The religious people also invited Jesus to their feasts, but it seems they always came with hidden agendas. Perhaps they wanted to drop names, to impress others by having the famous teacher grace their dining-room table. Or, more likely, they wanted to find subtle ways to tear at Jesus' reputation and discredit him, maybe even bring formal charges against him.

Wherever Jesus went, the religious people were always there, spying on him, making sure he behaved, and trying to figure out why he associated with all the wrong people—tax collectors and sinners, as the watchdogs of purity and piety usually called them.

This day the religious watchdogs grumbled openly, saying in Jesus' presence, "This fellow welcomes sinners and eats with them" (Luke 15:2). But Jesus did not let the religious elite wreck the party. He just kept right on celebrating and at the same time called on the spoilsports to reconsider their attitudes. How nice it would be if they could truly join the party.

How did Jesus call on them to rethink their attitudes? He did it, as he did so often, by telling stories, parables that challenged and provoked the hearers. This time Jesus used three parables to call his hearers to refashion their worldviews, to invite them to loosen up and enjoy the favor of their loving heavenly Father. The only problem was, the religious elite didn't even know their heavenly Father was loving. They thought of God more as a stingy and demanding boss. At least that's how Jesus characterized them in the third story he told that day.

The first story Jesus told was of a shepherd who loved his flock so much that even though he had ninety-nine well-behaved sheep that stayed in the pen where they belonged, he wasn't satisfied until he had found the one sheep that had gone astray. When he found it he threw a great party that cost him far more than the one sheep he could have left out there in the cold. Who cares? He loved his sheep so much, he was willing to kill the fatted calf to celebrate the herd that was complete again.

I think the religious people loved that story, at least the part about them being so well behaved and safe and secure in the fold. But the perceptive ones might have been bothered by the story a bit too. The shepherd stood for God, of course. The lost sheep was someone who did not follow the law, of course. Well, that would mean the party at the end was grossly overdone. They sure hoped Jesus was not trying to justify his present carousing with all those sinners.

Before they could put it all together, Jesus had another story for them. This time it was a woman with ten coins. Trouble is, one had disappeared somehow, and she wouldn't stop hunting until she had scoured the whole place. But when she found it, she promptly blew the whole piggy bank to throw a party with her friends. That's how happy she was to find the one lost coin. Perhaps the Pharisees were scratching their heads a bit harder by now. A woman couldn't possible stand for God. How can anyone love a coin that much? Surely Jesus wouldn't be in favor of loving money that much. What a waste! It'd be better to leave the coin lost than spend all ten for a party. And why is Jesus always talking about parties anyway?

But they had little time to figure that one out before Jesus started on story number 3 to show that God was not satisfied with the return of a lost son. God also wanted to win back the son who never left home.

What's in the Name?

Tradition has dubbed this story "the prodigal son." I think it got its name from the Pharisees, or maybe from church people who share some of their faults. For it is hard to think of a less appropriate name. It's as though Jesus were telling a story so that everyone would recognize how bad one of the boys in this family was, or as though he cared only about the faults of the younger son, who confessed them, and not of the older son, who didn't, or as though he didn't really mean to highlight the loving father at all, when in fact he is the only character who is there at the beginning, in the middle, and at the end, always expressing his tremendous love for both of his boys, even though both of them abused it and only one confessed his fault.

Most of us know the general lines of the story. It's about two sons, the younger one chomping at the bit for some lively adventures, the older one slaving away at home and complaining about his hard work, his boring existence, his wasteful brother, and his far too generous father. The younger son was driven to repentance when his money ran out and he was left friendless and hungry, working for a pig farmer. The older son never did repent;

he just complained. But the father never stopped looking out for the returning adventurer and never stopped reaching out to the hard-working, critical older son. The story ends without ending. The father is still appealing to his older son to come join the party. But we don't know what he'll decide.

That's how Jesus leaves it with the Pharisees as well. They felt good at first. Surely they were among the ninety-nine sheep that never went astray. Perhaps they felt almost as good to be considered among the nine coins that never got lost. But in the third story there was only one alternative to the sinful so-called prodigal. Surely Jesus wasn't comparing them to the older brother. Surely Jesus didn't believe their hearts also needed changing.

We know this story so well that it's hard to hear it in a new way. It is even more difficult to know how it applies to us, especially if we're sure we're not half as bad as the prodigal son.

I want us to consider a way of reading the story that might not have occurred to us before. Is this story really about a sinful son and all the wrongs he committed? The Pharisees would have loved to believe this story was really about how bad the younger son was and how badly he needed to repent. That way they wouldn't have to deal with the curve ball Jesus threw in at the end, the part about the older son, the part that called their own faithfulness into question.

What Did the Younger Son Do Wrong?

I want to suggest that this parable isn't about right and wrong at all, not if we measure right and wrong by some kind of objective legal standard or moral code. I was once fascinated to encounter research indicating that we can't be sure the younger son broke a single law. It wasn't against the law to ask for his share of the estate. The father could always say no if he wanted to.

It wasn't against the law to pack up and leave home. Well, as the modern translations make clear, he did more than pack a suitcase. Where he was going he had more use for cash than fields, so he sold everything and stashed the proceeds in his carry-on. But he didn't break any laws doing that. And it wasn't against the law to move to a distant country. Risky, maybe, but not illegal. Lots of young people move to new places.

He squandered his wealth in wild living. Clearly that wasn't prudent, but can we be sure he did anything illegal? Of course he should have shown better judgment. But did he really do anything that was technically illegal or immoral? Where's there a law that says you always have to be reasonable and plan ahead? Is it against the law to enjoy life a bit?

There is that one line about squandering his living on prostitutes. But how can we be sure he really did that? The line about prostitutes comes from the older brother. Did he really know what his brother had done with the money, or was he making that up? Can we trust the judgmental, self-righteous (and maybe just a little bit jealous) older brother to accurately describe how the prodigal son had lived?

Well, there probably was some truth in it. Even the younger son had to admit he wasn't spotless. But he could easily have found some defenses for his behavior, had he been so inclined. Still, whether he broke laws or not, his life hit the skids eventually.

At exactly the time he ran out of money, a severe famine came over the whole country. Sure, he should have prepared for the possibility, but how could he know that there would be an economic downturn? We can't blame the younger son for the famine, can we?

The part about the pigs would have been a disgrace for a Jew, but he wasn't eating the meat. They wouldn't even give him the slop the pigs were eating.

If we really look closely, it's hard to prove that the younger son actually broke any laws. So why does he confess from the bottom of his heart, "Father, I have sinned against heaven and against you"?

It's All About Relationships

I think the answer is that he understood what really counts in the family of God. What counts above all is relationships. According to Jesus, these count far more than how technically right or wrong a person lives—more, for that matter, than slaving away for the father "all these years." Carrying out commands is not the bottom line. This is what the older brother apparently never understood. He challenged his father with the claim, "For all these years I have been working like a slave for you and I have never disobeyed your command" (v. 29). Maybe he was right, but unfortunately for him, that simply didn't count for much. Relationships are the important thing.

Let's look at the parable again. Instead of asking which laws were broken, what if we asked which relationships were abused? Then the parable looks different. Then neither of the sons can have much with which to defend themselves. To ask for one's share of the estate didn't break any law, but it was still an unimaginable thing to do. It was as if the young man were complaining to his father, "You are living too long. I don't want to wait any longer. I want to get something out of life *now*. I don't want to wait until you're dead."

The older brother didn't do much better when he later complained, "*All these years* I have been working like a slave for you." "Look how long I've been waiting to become the boss. How much longer do you intend to live, Dad?" The issue is not obeying commands. The issue is relationships, and the relationship to their father was disdained by both of the sons.

The relationship between the two sons was no better. The older son accuses his father, "When this son of yours came back, who has devoured your property with prostitutes, you killed the fatted calf for him!" "This son of yours"—as if he wanted to make things clear—"he's not my brother, not anymore. If you haven't rejected him by now, I sure have."

Of course, the younger son kind of deserved this rejection.

Both sons knew what would happen if the inheritance was divided after the death of the father. The older brother would get two portions and the younger son only one. The inheritance laws regulated that. Both knew as well that when a father decided to divide the property while he was still alive, it was so that he could divide things fifty-fifty. The younger son had dared to beg for that, so he ended up with a considerably larger portion of the inheritance than he would have otherwise. He hadn't actually broken a law, but he had sure put a strain on family relationships.

What about the other things he did, such as selling the land, moving away, wasting the property? That was unheard of in his culture. If a father chose to divide the property while he was still alive, it was taken for granted that the son would support his parents in their old age. It was so taken for granted that they didn't even need laws to regulate it.

Both sons had acted disgracefully. The difference between them was that the younger son recognized what he had done and came back to repent. This parable is not finally about how terrible things can become for those who fall into sin. It is rather about how important it is to preserve loving relationships and, when necessary, to rebuild the ones that break down.

We've always known that this parable portrays a young man who sinned immeasurably, reached the bottom, and was totally dependent on the forgiveness of a loving father. But exactly how he sinned and what it meant to hit the bottom is where our thinking is challenged by the parable. In terms of breaking laws, the son was far less guilty than we might suppose. Where he fell short was in relationships. That's surely why his confession acknowledged his sin "against heaven and before you." The issue is not objective guilt but broken relationships.

If this parable is going to speak to us, we need to move beyond questions of objective guilt. If the parable provokes us only to ask what we've done wrong or which laws we've broken, we will escape the force of it. It turns out to be about other people—prodigals, down-and-outers, ultra-legalists. But if we ask the far more important questions about how things are between me and my God, between me and my brothers and sisters, then this parable can still confront and challenge us and, depending on our response, condemn or console us.

Of course, for most Christians it is more comfortable to divert the whole topic to moral correctness. It's so much easier to maintain blamelessness before the law or to measure how hard we have slaved in the fields as the older brother did. But we run the risk of siding with the Pharisees. Remember, it was the tax collectors and sinners who were enjoying the party with Jesus.

When we focus on the law, we're constantly tempted to say, "I never once disobeyed your command." If we focus on relationships, we are invited to say, "Father, I have sinned against heaven and against you." When we say that, God throws a party for us.

We have examined the parable as though it is about two sons struggling with priorities and struggling to discover what the father never doubts from beginning to end. The right priorities must be relationships in God's family. That's why the father works so lovingly and patiently to restore the relationships that have broken down.

The Father

The usual name of this parable, the prodigal son, effectively marginalizes the father. When we see that everything revolves around relationships, the father is restored to center stage. Some have tried to centralize the father in the parable by titling it the parable of the waiting father. But is it not rather a parable about a *running* father?

How far was this father willing to go to restore the broken relationships in his family? Here we get some help from Kenneth Bailey. As a professor at the Hebrew University in Jerusalem, he interpreted the parables so that they might speak to his students and his Muslim teaching colleagues. As a missionary to Arab peasants, he sought to preach the gospel in the small farming villages around Jerusalem.

The parable of the prodigal son was one that Bailey used often to share the good news of Jesus. Many rural Arabs have a culture today that is remarkably similar to the culture of the Jews in Jesus' day. Bailey sometimes gained insights into the significance of this parable from the Arab farmers with whom he shared the gospel, insights he could never have gained in the university library.

As he shared the parable, Bailey would watch his hearers responses closely. To them it was self-evident that this parable was about relationships. These people were not asking whether it was legal for the younger son to ask for his share of the inheritance. They wondered how a son could bring such shame on himself and his family. How could he take advantage of family relationships like that?

And so it went through the entire story. But the biggest surprise of all was the reaction Bailey observed as he told of the father running to meet the returning prodigal. His hearers wondered why the father too would bring shame on himself.

"How's that?" asked Bailey.

"Because an old man wouldn't run."

"Why not?"

"Because he would have to lift up his robe."

Suddenly Bailey found an answer to a question that had troubled him. His Muslim colleagues at the university in Jerusalem had often challenged his claim that God's forgiveness was a costly thing, paid for by God's own grace. They had often replied with this parable. The father simply pronounced a word of forgiveness, and it didn't cost him anything.

Now Bailey understood something new. The prodigal son was on his way back home. What could he expect from the people of the village? They would mock him, laugh at him, and scorn him. The children would throw stones or spit at him; some would turn their backs. This young man would never again have a place in the village.

But the people of the village saw something totally unexpected. The father who was so scorned by his younger son did something himself that would make *him* a laughingstock. He made a fool of himself by picking up his garments and running. That was unheard of for a man his age in that culture. Now the children would mock him too.

And so these two, father and son, come together back into the village, both objects of scorn. The father was willing to sacrifice his own honor so that his son would not have to come home alone in disgrace. Bailey gained new insight not only into this parable but also into the whole New Testament message of grace. Grace is a loving God taking on our shame and exchanging it for glory.

Yes, it did cost God something: honor, which is what the parable is ultimately about. It is about a prodigal son recognizing the priority of relationships. But even more it is about a Father for whom relationships are so important that he's willing to risk his honor, submit to scorn, and break all the rules of propriety if only relationships with prodigals can be rebuilt.

A Generous Waste

Have you ever thought about the word *prodigal?* It means "generously wasteful," and so we apply it to the younger son who lived his frivolous life and wasted his money on things that really didn't count and in the end didn't make him happy either. Sometimes we apply it to the older brother, who by slaving and complaining wasted a perfectly good opportunity to enjoy the love and security of a wonderful home, not to mention the parties.

Have you ever thought of calling this the parable of the prodigal father? What a generous waste to kill a fatted calf to celebrate one little lamb that is found. What a generous waste to spend ten coins on a party to celebrate finding one that was lost.

What a generous waste to throw a party for a son who had just frittered away half your fortune on, well, nothing really. But God is like that.

The father is willing to throw away his honor if necessary to welcome a returning son. He'll come begging a self-righteous son to quit working so hard and join the music and dancing. And he'll do it even if there's not much chance the son will actually come. What a waste! But if even one sheep is found, one coin is found, one child comes home, well, he would spend his whole fortune to make that happen. That's just how God is.

What a perfect parable for Jesus to tell while eating with tax collectors and sinners. What a perfect parable to challenge and confront in all cultures and all centuries, as long as there are people who scorn a relationship with God—as long as there are people still learning that such a relationship is infinitely more important to God than being technically morally correct or slaving away in our father's fields.

A loving relationship with us is more important to God than God's own honor and all the rules of propriety. And God waits patiently until a loving relationship with our Father is more important to us than defending *our* honor. It's more important than being good, more important than slaving away for God, more important than pursuing a kind of happiness that leaves us empty and unfulfilled while all the treasures of heaven are waiting for us to enjoy.

To be sure, this parable speaks to the down-and-outers who have hit bottom, grasping for anything that might mean the rescue of a ruined life. There's good news here for those who feel like the younger son starving near the pigs' trough. It speaks to those whose wasteful and frivolous lifestyles haven't caught up with them yet but who have a deep longing for something better than the kind of happiness they are so desperately chasing. For such people there's good news here. It also speaks to those who stand up proudly claiming they never disobeyed a single command and then complain about those who work less, spend more, or enjoy life more easily. Maybe some of us fit fairly well into this category. If so, there's good news for us here.

But surely this parable also has a powerful message for those of us who find ourselves somewhere between those extremes, somewhere between very good and very bad, somewhere between lost and found, somewhere between the pig troughs in a foreign land and living at the center of God's loving family. Wherever we are on any of these scales, there is good news for us here. God is saying to us, "I'm ready to throw another party. Just give me half a reason and we'll kill the fatted calf!"

Whenever we take just one step toward home, we can be sure our loving Father will come running toward us. He'll throw his arms around us, welcome us home, put a ring on our finger, and put shoes on our feet. And there'll be a party in our honor!

Discussion Questions

1. With which character in this parable can I identify most easily? Why?

2. In our congregation, is it clear that reconciled and healthy relationships are more important than behaving correctly in relation to the law?

3. How does this parable challenge us to reexamine or even correct our idea of what God is like?

For Further Reading

Bailey, Kenneth. *The Cross and the Prodigal.* St. Louis: Concordia, 1973.

Nouwen, Henri. *The Return of the Prodigal Son: A Story of Homecoming.* New York: Image, 1993.

11

A Pile of Stones or a Word of Grace

In this final chapter we examine John 8:2-11, an episode in which Jesus stands alongside an adulteress and takes a stand against her legalistic judges. As Christian churches we can learn from this event how to choose the risk of grace over the security of legalism.

Dangerous or Beautiful?

In this fascinating story, a woman is caught in the act of adultery, and the religious people want to get Jesus' approval for their plan to stone her. Jesus' response to the religious leaders leaves them speechless. And his response to the woman? He has no stones for her, just a word of grace.

This is a familiar story, made familiar by the memorable matching of wits between Jesus and a group of Pharisees. He, as always, outwits them. But the importance of this story is not its cleverness; it is in the unbelievable extension of grace to a sinner when the religious experts of the day want to mete out only punishment.

In most Bibles, there is a note attached to this account that usually says, "The earliest and most reliable manuscripts do not have this text." Why is this text found in some old manuscripts of the Bible but not in others? Well, there are two possibilities.

Either some manuscripts left it out or other manuscripts sneaked it in. But why would anyone take it out? Did they perhaps think it was too dangerous? What if Christians thought Jesus was saying adultery is not that big a deal? What if they thought he was almost permitting it? On the other hand, why would anyone add this story if it was not original? Maybe they thought the story was just too beautiful to lose.

Is this story too dangerous to keep or too beautiful to lose? Maybe our answer depends on whether we identify more easily with the woman or with the religious people. I personally think the story is too beautiful to lose. Here is Jesus, the merciful one, who stands on the side of sinners and makes new beginnings possible.

The Characters

We want to begin our examination of this text by paying attention to the various characters, starting with those in the crowd, who were curious and eager to hear Jesus preach. That day the crowd heard Jesus speak only one sentence to the religious leaders and carry on a very brief conversation with the woman. That's all. Yet I suspect they learned more about Jesus and his ways that day than they could have learned in many a sermon.

Then there are the scribes and Pharisees—proud, self-righteous, insincere. They were the guardians of holiness, or so they wanted people to think. Jesus did not think of them as holy. He described them mostly as hypocrites. This time they did not come to uphold righteousness. They came to set a trap for Jesus. It was clever and well carried out, but it was not good enough to catch Jesus. Today he will be the one who sets the best trap.

Then there is the adulteress, who was dragged in by the religious men. Poor woman. Not to say that she was without sin. Jesus himself told her later to go and sin no more. She was not innocent; nevertheless she was a victim in a hypocritical plot. We are left wondering whether she was even given a chance to get dressed before being dragged into the crowd. If she was not physically exposed, she was surely stripped of her dignity. "Caught in the very act" (v. 4)—the whole crowd had heard it.

And then there is Jesus. What will sincere, loving, accepting, gracious Jesus do with this woman, a sinner and yet a helpless victim? What will Jesus, who can smell hypocrisy from a mile away, do with these religious people?

The characters are all there, except one. There is somebody missing—the man. It takes two to commit adultery. Where is the man? Why is he not there? We are left wondering.

The Trap

"Teacher," the scribes and Pharisees begin, though they cannot honestly claim a desire to learn anything from him. "This woman was caught in the very act of committing adultery" (v. 4). Then, as if Jesus didn't know it, they explain that "Moses commanded us to stone such women." And then the question with which they hope to catch Jesus: "Now what do you say?" (v. 5).

It seemed a perfect trap. If Jesus said to stone her, he would lose his good reputation for taking the side of sinners, outcasts, and others rejected by the religious establishment. He had eaten with them, proclaimed God's forgiveness, and invited them to follow him. The crowds loved him because he was merciful and stood up to those who would rather reject, judge, and punish them.

If he replied against stoning her, the crowds could easily imagine that he did not consider adultery a serious matter. It might look as though Jesus were saying that the Old Testament law did not need to be taken seriously. To set himself up against God's law would make him a lawbreaker and the religious leaders could claim the right to stone him along with the woman—or perhaps instead of the woman, for Jesus was the one they were really after. It was a perfect trap, indeed.

Jesus also faced another dilemma: he would have to decide between Moses and Rome. What Moses had said was perfectly clear: "If a man commits adultery with the wife of his neighbor, both the adulterer and the adulteress shall be put to death" (Leviticus 20:10). But Rome had taken the right to practice capital punishment away from the Jews. Only the Romans could execute lawbreakers, and they did not do so by stoning, nor did they crucify adulterers.

So if Jesus said, "Don't stone her," he would be complying with Rome but disobeying Moses, which would be religiously dangerous. To approve of stoning the woman, he'd be obeying the Law of Moses but ignoring the law of Rome, which would be politically dangerous. Either way the religious leaders would have what they wanted—grounds for condemning him.

How will Jesus walk out of this one? It is a dangerous situation for him. If he does not step carefully, he will surely slip into one of the many pitfalls surrounding him. He is also confronted with an unusual situation—not because adultery was rare, but because it was very difficult to meet the conditions that had been laid down under Jewish law for carrying out the death sentence.

Here were the conditions: There had to have been two witnesses. Both had to have seen the deed with their own eyes. An educated guess as to what had happened did not count. Furthermore, the reports of the two witnesses had to agree to the last detail. If not, the witnesses themselves would be in trouble with the law.

It is not hard to see why adulterers were seldom condemned to death. It was almost impossible to meet the strict conditions. Where would they find two witnesses who had seen everything? That is why some interpreters suspect that the entire episode was a trap, not only for Jesus, but for the woman as well. The entire affair must have been secretly arranged and secretly observed.

That would also explain something about the offending man not being there. Maybe he was there! Perhaps the Pharisees hired the unscrupulous adulterer, or maybe one of them volunteered for the job. We do not know all the details, but they apparently had the two required witnesses who had seen the whole thing and were prepared to testify under oath about it. The absence of the man is easy to explain if we imagine that the entire episode from start to finish was a carefully contrived plot to get Jesus.

Jesus' Response

At first Jesus says nothing. Instead he stoops and writes on the ground. What does he write? We simply do not know, even though we are very tempted to guess:

- Is he simply buying a little time, trying to listen as his heavenly Father tells him what to do?
- Is he perhaps writing the law on the ground, to show that he knows the law just as well as his enemies?
- Is he perhaps making a list of the sins of these religious men?
- Is he writing the name of the secret adulterer, or maybe the unscrupulous witnesses?

Jesus knows how to spring the trap back on his opponents and use it to reveal their own hypocrisy. They are pressing him for an answer, and he gives one: "Let anyone among you who is without sin be the first to throw a stone at her" (v. 7).

Imagine the intensity of the situation. Those in the crowd are holding their breath. What now? The Pharisees are getting more nervous by the second. The woman is anxiously waiting, full of fear. What will happen now?

Gradually the situation becomes clear to everyone. Jesus has simply walked away from the trap. He has neither condemned the woman nor allowed the sin; he has disobeyed neither Moses nor Rome; and he has maintained his reputation as the merciful and obedient one. Jesus turned the trap around on his opponents. Now *they* are caught: Anyone without sin? In this group?

The oldest ones, no doubt the wisest ones, recognize the danger they face in the midst of the crowd, which sees Jesus as a hero who can read thoughts and reveal the secrets of the heart. One by one they sneak away, knowing that if they do not disappear quickly, if they claim to be without sin after their scheming, they are really asking for trouble. And so one whole set of characters disappears from the scene. But the drama is not over. The woman is still standing there with Jesus, and a huge crowd still needs to learn something from him. Jesus speaks to her: "Woman, where are they? Has no one condemned you?" She replies, "No one, sir" (vv. 10-11).

Will the condemnation come now from Jesus? After all, the one without sin is standing in front of her. According to the condition he has laid down, he has full right to carry out the death penalty. But Jesus came not to condemn sinners but to save them. He came to bring God's grace, not God's judgment. He came to give a new chance and new life.

"Neither do I condemn you. Go your way, and from now on do not sin again" (v. 11b).

But what about the death penalty? Does sin have no consequences? Does a simple word of forgiveness wipe the slate clean? No, things are not that simple. In fact the anger of those ready to stone this woman will be let loose on Jesus, who pronounces her forgiven. They desire her death today, but soon they will be demanding his. Jesus, who stood up for this woman, will soon stand in her place. He will accept the anger and rejection; he will bear the sin. And he will do the same for all who have ever read this woman's story. "Indeed, God did not send the Son into the world to condemn the world, but in order that the world might be saved through him" (John 3:17).

She was guilty, and so are we. "Go your way, and from now on do not sin again," Jesus said to her. He says the same to us. Yet he also assured her, "Neither do I condemn you." Jesus takes the judgment on himself that we might receive God's grace. That is the good news. God loved us so much "that he gave his only Son, so that everyone who believes in him may not perish but may have eternal life" (3:16).

God sent Jesus so that this life could be offered to everyone, to adulterers and adulteresses, to scribes and Pharisees, to everyone in that temple crowd on that day in Jerusalem and to all of you reading this book today. How powerfully this story about the adulteress woman proclaims the good news!

We too are sometimes hypocritical and judgmental, sometimes adulterers and adulteresses, sometimes selfish or greedy or proud or complacent. If Jesus said today, "Let the one without sin pick up the first stone," none of us would have any greater right to throw stones than did the Pharisees.

Reading this text today, each of us has to take our stand with one of the characters in the story. Will we try to sneak out of the trap like the Pharisees? Will we stand at a distance, curious but uninvolved like the crowd? Or will we stand with the woman, knowing that Jesus knows all about us and has every right to cast the first stone—but hearing his words of grace?

This woman's story is the story of all those who have received God's grace. It can become the story of all those who have not yet opened their hands and hearts to receive it from a merciful Jesus, who stands with sinners and offers to them the grace of God.

Dangerous Grace

This story is a little dangerous too. It is dangerous to say, "Neither do I condemn you," to adulterers, adulteresses, sinners of every kind. What if the church that Jesus established said that? "Neither do we condemn you." If people no longer face any consequences for their sinful choices, what motivation is left to be faithful followers of Jesus?

I want to close by asking you to use your imagination with me. We know that only a short time after Jesus spoke his words of grace to this adulteress woman, a huge crowd was heard crying, "Crucify him!" Lots of people were calling for Jesus' death. The very people who had celebrated Jesus now turned their backs on him and sided with his enemies.

Try to imagine who might have been in that crowd crying, "Crucify him!" Might there have been some people who had seen him do miracles? Jesus did not do his miracles in secret. He had been famous as a miracle worker, but it was also as a miracle worker that he was condemned. No doubt many people who had observed the miracles turned against him in the end.

Were there some who had heard him preach? I imagine just about every person who called for Jesus' death had heard him preach. They not only rejected the miracle worker, they rejected the preacher as well.

What about his followers? If Judas, who had followed Jesus for three years, could turn against him, then surely others turned too.

How about the woman caught in adultery? Do you think she was there too, yelling, "Crucify him," a few weeks after Jesus had said, "Neither do I condemn you." Would she turn around and call for Jesus' death?

I cannot imagine it, because deep in my heart, deep in our hearts, we know that the most powerful way of drawing people to Jesus is not with miracles or sermons or calls to be faithful disciples. It is by sharing God's matchless grace. That is why pouring out God's grace on sinners was the highest priority of Jesus' ministry. And I think that one of the highest priorities of the church should be sharing the gospel that offers grace to sinners. We have received grace freely, and we freely pass it on to others who deserve only judgment. After all, we too are among those who have been given grace we did not deserve and spared the judgment we did deserve.

This is a dangerous story if we want to abuse God's grace, misunderstand it, or take it for granted. But it is a life-changing story if we are ready to receive God's grace and let it change our lives. Jesus chose grace over a pile of stones. We're invited to receive that grace and called to pass it on.

Discussion Questions

1. In your opinion, was this story "too dangerous to keep" or "too beautiful to lose" for the early copyists? Which is it for us?

2. What are your reactions when Jesus pours out grace in situations in which we humans are more likely to condemn?

3. Where and how can the church concretely follow Jesus' example of grace-giving?

For Further Reading

Augsburger, David. *Caring Enough to Forgive: True Forgiveness.* Scottdale: Herald Press, 1981.

Yancey, Philip. *What's So Amazing About Grace?* Grand Rapids, MI: Zondervan, 1997.

Bottom Lines

Over the past twenty years, as I have led seminars for churches or associations, the most commonly requested themes have been the very themes of this book: biblical interpretation, the nature of the church, and ethics. I have come to the conclusion that none can really be addressed adequately without addressing all three at the same time.

Biblical interpretation impacts the church and its ethics. All faithful biblical interpretation requires that the texts be read in the Christian community. Faithful biblical interpretation must eventually lead to the primary ethical question, how should God's people live in this world as representatives of God's kingdom?

Our understanding of church requires biblical input and leads to ethical output. The Bible is not taken seriously by a church that views itself as merely a support system for individualized spirituality. In Scripture, the community, not the individual, is central to God's plan. The community is the primary agent for interpreting Scripture and bearing witness to God's kingdom. The church departs from biblical norms when it centralizes doctrine or spiritual experience and minimizes faithful living, witness, and service.

Christian ethics are discerned and developed by processing biblical input within the local church. The Bible does not answer all our ethical questions, but it provides the framework within which discerning bodies of believers discover God's will. While we can learn from trained ethicists and from biblical scholars, the concrete work of ethical discernment belongs to each community of believers that seeks to live faithfully in its cultural context.

ዺ

This book is about the Bible, it is about the church, and it is about ethics, three things that are often held separately. But it provides something I believe is absolutely necessary. There are already too many books claiming that careful textual analysis is the only thing needed in order to extract unchanging ethical guidelines from God's Word, as though one clever scholar can pronounce for all people everywhere God's will on a given subject. No wonder most books on ethical issues actually set out to refute others aiming to do the same thing! The church is not well served by mutually contradictory attempts to defend a correct, once-for-all biblical view on an ethical issue. It is better served by a climate in which personal viewpoints can be articulated without fear of rejection. It is better served if it learns to distinguish between shared convictions that define our core identity and diverse opinions that challenge all of us to keep learning, if it practices gracious acceptance of more than one narrow perspective, and if it learns where and when and how compromises can be reached that preserve church unity and enhance the church's witness. This book aims to help the church learn these important skills and priorities.

The ideas in *All Right Now* have been taking shape for twenty years. I have often come home from a seminar and been met by my wife with the inevitable question, "How did it go?" Most times, the answer is something like this: "It think it went really well. I learned some new things, and I believe the participants in the seminar were able to see some things from a new perspective. It was a worthwhile day together, and I think it will make a difference in the future."

But on a few occasions it did not turn out like that. I remember vividly the two-hour drive home after a series of meetings in a church that was coming apart at the seams, unable to resolve differences over an ethical question. I agonized how I would answer my wife's inevitable question. I'd be lying if I said it had gone well. Truth is, I was convinced that the church was sorry it had invited me to help it work through its issue. I had interpreted the Scriptures with such care; I had worked out what I thought was a great solution to their dilemma; I had presented it with all the clarity and conviction I could muster. At the end of two long evenings together, the two sides still disagreed with each other. But now both sides also disagreed with me, and nobody knew where to turn next. It was a long ride home.

I walked in the door and preempted my wife's question with my own. "Would you still love me if I said it did not go well?" She said she would, of course, and she helped me over my discouragement. That was the day I went into labor with this book. I became convinced that far more important than proclaiming the "right" answer to a church in conflict is helping the church learn how to listen and learn and discern and decide. If the church then ends up deciding differently than I would have, I can rejoice that they have learned to do what God assigned them to do.

Since then I have experienced the same phenomenon in my own congregation. We struggled for eighteen months with an ethical issue. In the end, we learned to listen and discern and decide, and to move on in unity, even though the decision ultimately made was not the one many in the congregation would have chosen. We studied the Scriptures together, we practiced being and becoming an ethically discerning Christian community, and we made a decision that enabled us to move on with mutual acceptance and enthusiasm for what God was doing among us and through us. "It has seemed good to the Holy Spirit and to us!"

I suppose it would flatter my ego if I learned that the individual chapters of this book led readers to agree with the positions I recommended. But the real goal of the book will not have been reached if that happens. It will have been reached if more and more local congregations discover their great privilege and responsibility to be an ethically discerning community, and if they learn a few tips that will help them effectively utilize the resources of Scripture, process these in their local contexts, and do it all in an attitude that reflects those illustrated in the final three chapters of this book. If that happens, I will rejoice—even if those congregations answer their ethical questions differently than I would have.

Notes

1. Walter Brueggemann, *Texts Under Negotiation: The Bible and Postmodern Imagination* (Minneapolis: Fortress Press, 1993), 19.

2. E. Stanley Jones, *The Christ of the Mount* (Nashville: Abingdon Press, 1981), 12-13.

3. Walter Wink, *Engaging the Powers: Discernment and Resistance in a World of Domination* (Minneapolis: Fortress Press, 1992), 175-84.

4. Richard Hays, *The Moral Vision of the New Testament* (San Francisco: Harper, 1996), 391.

5. H. Wayne House, ed., *Divorce and Remarriage: Four Christian Views* (Downers Grove, IL: InterVarsity Press, 1990).

6. The names of the people in this story have been changed.

7. See *The Church and Human Sexuality: A Lutheran Perspective: First Draft of a Social Statement* (Chicago: Division for Church in Society, Department for Studies of the Evangelical Lutheran Church in America, 1993).

8. Richard Hays, *The Moral Vision of the New Testament* (San Francisco: Harper, 1996), 382.

9. *Ibid.*, 400.

10. C. S. Lewis, *Mere Christianity* (London: Collins, 1952), 188.

The Author

Timothy J. Geddert is professor of New Testament at Mennonite Brethren Biblical Seminary and adjunct professor at the Theologischer Seminar Bienenberg in Liestal, Switzerland. He has lived and taught at various times in Germany, and the first version of *All Right Now* was published in German. He has worked as a church planter, pastor, and teacher in many countries, including Canada, the United States, and Germany. Geddert is  the author of numerous books, including the Believers Church Bible Commentary on *Mark* and *Watchwords: Mark 13 in Markan Eschatology*. He was born in Saskatoon, Saskatchewan, and is the father of six children. He and his wife, Gertrud, live in Fresno, California.